IMAGES OF BASEBALL

BASEBALL AT BALL STATE

From 1928 through 1970, Ball State's baseball games were played on the diamond next to the Cardinals' football field. The track that ran around the football field extended into the outfield. On the left of the baseball diamond is Christy Woods, and across University Avenue on the right is Ball Memorial Hospital.

Paul Beauchamp "Billy" Williams served as Ball State's baseball coach for 35 seasons between 1922 and 1958, compiling a record of 207-228-4. He took a leave in 1927, and there were no intercollegiate athletics at Ball State in 1944 due to World War II.

IMAGES OF BASEBALL

BASEBALL AT BALL STATE

John Ginter

ARCADIA
PUBLISHING

ISBN 978-0-7385-2301-9

Published by Arcadia Publishing
Charleston, South Carolina

Printed in the United States of America.

Library of Congress Catalog Card Number: 2002094830

For all general information contact Arcadia Publishing at:
Telephone 843-853-2070
Fax 843-853-0044
E-Mail sales@arcadiapublishing.com
For customer service and orders:
Toll-Free 1-888-313-2665

Visit us on the Internet at www.arcadiapublishing.com

This book is dedicated to all coaches, players and fans of Ball State baseball—past and future—and to my family, especially my wife, Marilyn, who insists I never again take on such a project.

Coach Rich Maloney and Bryan Bullington listen to a question from the media during a press conference after the Pittsburgh Pirates made the pitcher the No. 1 overall selection in the 2002 Major League Baseball draft. In Maloney's seven years as the Cardinals' coach, 22 of his players were drafted, including two in the first round.

CONTENTS

ACKNOWLEDGMENTS

I can do all things through Christ, who strengtheneth me.

—Phillippians 4:13.

This book would not have become a reality without the strengths of many generous people who made critical contributions to its creation. Starting at the beginning, the idea for this book sprang from Dr. Don Park, Ball State's vice president of University Advancement, and he also made worthwhile suggestions about its context. My mentor at the outset of the research and planning was Dr. Bruce E. Geelhoed, director of the Center for Middletown Studies. John Straw, archives and special collections librarian at Ball State, and his staff were cooperative and efficient in providing many of the photographs of the early years of Cardinals and Hoosieroons baseball.

Most of the remainder of the pictures and much of the information for this book came from Ball State's Athletics Communications Office through the cooperation of assistant athletics director Joe Hernandez, a former BSU baseball student manager. His secretary, Robin Brown, was incredibly helpful and patient in fulfilling the seemingly endless requests this book required. Her tireless efforts were critical for this project to be completed, and the author's appreciation for her cannot be overstated. Brad Caudill, assistant director of athletics communications, who works with the Ball State baseball program, also provided information, as did other members of that office's staff. The author also thanks Earl Yestingsmeier for his meticulous record-keeping during his years as sports information director. Special commendation must go to Bob Moore, former assistant director of athletics communications, because his compilation of baseball data during his years working with the program was incredibly helpful.

The assistance and aid of John Huffer, coordinator of photographic services at Ball State, was crucial to this book's illustrations. Not only did John take many of the pictures that appear in these pages, but he also provided his talents in many other ways toward the pictorial portions of the book. Also adding technical support in the preparation of the book was Ken Johnson, director of Printing Services at Ball State. Ed Shipley, executive director of alumni programs at Ball State, and his staff provided assistance with historical data.

The author is also grateful for those who provided much of the human interest portions of this book. Those people include former coaches Ray Louthen, Bob Rickel (also a former player) and Pat Quinn and former players Gabor Takats, Ted Huber and Bryan Bullington.

The author thanks his daughters, Tammy Bibbs and Kindra Johns, along with long time family friend Janie Taylor for their proofreading efforts.

And finally, I want to express my appreciation to my wife, Marilyn, who performed many duties and assignments in her normally efficient manner throughout the creation of this book. Her love and caring also were important as this book moved from beginning to end.

INTRODUCTION

Ball State pitcher Bryan Bullington's selection by the Pittsburgh Pirates as the No. 1 pick in the 2002 Major League Baseball draft culminated Rich Maloney's seven-year coaching reign, during which the Cardinals became dominant in the Mid-American Conference, highly respected in the Midwest and well known throughout the nation. During the Maloney era, Ball State won three Mid-American Conference championships and four MAC West titles while producing 22 draft selections, including two first-round choices—Bullington and future Major Leaguer Larry Bigbie—and two others who were supplemental picks between the first and second rounds. But while the Cardinals enjoyed unprecedented success under Maloney, the Ball State baseball program boasts a rich history that spans more than eight decades.

Orville Sink began the baseball program in 1919, the first year of the institution, which was then known as the Eastern Division of the Indiana State Normal School. After basketball was introduced at the institution in the winter of 1918-19, baseball in the spring became the second sport at the school, which was established to educate teachers. The school's first baseball team competed against local high school and independent squads, but no records of the outcomes exist.

Paul B. (Billy) Williams became Ball State's coach three years later and remained in the post

In 1917, Muncie National Institute had its final baseball team before the school closed the next fall. Later in the year, the Ball brothers bought the buildings and grounds of the school, and the following year, the Eastern Division of the Indiana State Normal School was established. The building behind the team is now the Administration Building for Ball State University.

through 1958, except for the 1927 season, when Norman Wann replaced him as Williams took a leave. Williams' most productive seasons were 1939 with a 12-3 record and 1936 with an 11-4 mark. Williams, however, contributed more than his coaching abilities to Ball State. In November of 1927, the Ball State school newspaper sponsored a contest to select a new nickname for its athletic teams to replace "Hoosieroons." A fan of the St. Louis Cardinals baseball team, Williams entered "Cardinals," which was chosen in a student vote. Williams won the $5 gold prize.

Succeeding Williams was Ray Louthen, who was Ball State's baseball coach from 1959 through 1970 and football coach from 1962 through 1967. Louthen recruited high school athletes to play both sports, and one of his best was Merv Rettenmund, who was drafted by the Dallas Cowboys as a running back but signed to play baseball for the Baltimore Orioles and spent parts of 13 seasons in the majors. Louthen led Ball State to National Collegiate Athletic Association playoff appearances in 1961, 1965 and 1969. In the 1969 NCAA regional, the Cardinals defeated both the Big Ten and Mid-American Conference champions on the same day. During Louthen's 12 years as Cardinals baseball coach, Ball State had its first two All-Americans—Ed Sherry and Jim Roudebush.

Upon Louthen's becoming athletic director at Ball State in 1970, he was succeeded by Bob Rickel, who played third base for Louthen's BSU squads from 1963 through 1965. Highlighting Rickel's 11 years at the Ball State helm was Ball State's entrance into the Mid-American Conference, one of the most important developments in the university's athletic history.

In 1983, Pat Quinn, a former bullpen catcher for the Cincinnati Reds who warmed up, among others, Hall of Fame pitcher Tom Seaver, became Ball State's sixth baseball coach and carried a professional expertise into the Cardinals' program. Three times under Quinn, Ball State finished fourth in the MAC race, but highlighting his 13 seasons as BSU's coach was the career of Thomas Howard, the 1986 Mid-American Conference Player of the Year and a first-team All-American who played portions of 11 seasons in the majors.

This book recalls the successful coaches, outstanding players, and great seasons that have been a part of Ball State baseball. But also on the following pages are stories that go beyond the facts and figures to make the history of Cardinal baseball come alive.

Orville Ernest Sink, professor of industrial arts and physical education at Indiana State Normal School, Eastern Division, began the school's baseball program in 1919 and coached the Hoosieroons on the diamond for three seasons.

One

Glory Days
Championships and NCAA Playoffs

May 30, 1969, has become known as the greatest day in Ball State baseball history. On that date, the Cardinals of Coach Ray Louthen defeated both the Big Ten and Mid-American Conference champions in the NCAA District 4 Playoffs at Minneapolis. But the afternoon finished with one of the biggest brawls in BSU baseball history, too.

After dropping a 15-6 decision to Southern Illinois the first day of the double-elimination tournament, Ball State rebounded the next afternoon with a 4-3 victory over Ohio University, the MAC champion. As the Cardinals were leaving the stadium, they passed the Minnesota players, who were on their way to the field to play Southern Illinois. Someone asked the Ball State team members who had won the first game, and one of the players answered, "We won." A Minnesota player quickly responded: "Oh, great. That's wonderful. We didn't want to play Ohio anyway." Animosity between Ball State and Minnesota players had begun.

It got worse during the game, as Minnesota fans shouted racial remarks at Ball State right fielder Pack Craig, an African-American. Finally, Craig called time out and headed toward the infield. Louthen met him near second base and immediately saw tears in the player's eyes. Craig said: "Coach, I can't stand it out there. Put me in left field or do something." Louthen asked what the problem was, and Craig answered: "They're calling me all kinds of names, and I can't stand that any longer. I'm going to go into the stands. I'll probably get the heck kicked out of me, but I've had all I can stand." An irate Louthen went to the first-base umpire, who was also African-American, and explained the situation. Louthen told the man in blue: "This kid is going back out there, and if they say anything to him again, we're walking off the field. It will probably be the first time in the history of the NCAA that a team is taken off the field because of racial slurs, but we'll walk off the field. You can do whatever you want." After huddling, the three umpires working the game went to the home dugout, and security was dispatched to the right-field area of the stands. Craig never heard any more derogatory remarks, but the tension between the teams had become more intense.

When Ball State got the final out of the 4-1 victory on a force-out at third base, the Cardinals rushed onto the field and Louthen ran to shake hands with Minnesota's third base coach. The Golden Gophers' player who had been out at third base jumped up, slapped down on the two coaches' hands as they were shaking and screamed, "Don't shake hands with those high school hot dogs." That was the final spark needed for a fight. Opposing players began swinging at each other. Fights erupted in many parts of the field. Louthen tried to grab players and throw them back toward the dugout while ducking punches himself. "It was a heck of a fight," he recalled. At least one player was left with a battle scar. Don Schmidt, a 5-foot-7-inch, 165-pound backup catcher from northwest Indiana who drove a beer truck before returning to school to finish his education, suffered a gash across his forehead. "He said he got it on some big guy's belt buckle when he was pounding the heck out of the Minnesota player in the stomach," Louthen said. Ball State was eliminated from the tournament the next day with a 4-3 loss to Southern Illinois, from which the Cardinals had swept a doubleheader on the last day of the regular season to earn the NCAA playoff berth.

Ball State also played in the NCAA District 4 Playoffs in 1965, suffering a 4-0 setback to Ohio State and a 4-3 loss to Detroit at Athens, Ohio. The Cardinals' only other NCAA bid came in 1961, when they played in the college division playoffs at Greencastle, Indiana, defeating Ohio Wesleyan by a 4-3 score and then dropping a 5-3 verdict to Southwestern (Tennessee) in the single-elimination event. Under Louthen, Ball State also won three Indiana Collegiate Conference championships.

The Cardinals' first league title came in the Indiana Intercollegiate Conference under coach Billy Williams. Ball State was a charter member of the Indiana Intercollegiate Conference, which was established in 1922. The Cardinals' first IIC baseball title in 1939 resulted from a critical doubleheader sweep at Hanover, then the league's baseball powerhouse, on May 15. Walter Pesavento pitched a shutout in the first game and Gabor Takats hit a home run as the Cardinals captured a 1-0 victory. Coach Williams figured Pesavento was throwing so well that he would start the right-hander in the second game, too. In the sixth inning of the seven-inning nightcap, Pesavento wore down. Hanover took the lead, but Ball State rallied for a 13-11 victory. "When we pulled out that game and won that championship," said Takats, the regular catcher in 1939, "that was the only time I saw Mr. Williams overcome with emotion. He had coached for a long time, and that was his first championship."

The Indiana Intercollegiate Conference became the Indiana Intercollegiate Athletic Association in 1949, but the following year, Ball State became a charter member of the Indiana Collegiate Conference. Under Louthen, Ball State won its first ICC title in 1961 and repeated the next season. The Cardinals added their third ICC title in 1965 before withdrawing from the league after the 1967-68 academic year.

Ball State was a major college independent for two years before joining with Indiana State, Illinois State, Southern Illinois and Northern Illinois to form the Conference of Midwestern Universities in 1971. That league survived two academic seasons before dissolving, and Ball State joined the Mid-American Conference in 1974. It wasn't until 1998, however, that the Cardinals won their first MAC title. Ball State added MAC championships in 1999 and 2001.

Outfielder Pack Craig made the NCAA All-Mideast third team in 1969 after hitting .313 for the Cardinals, who advanced to the NCAA District Four Playoffs. Craig also was chosen the most valuable player on the 1969 Ball State team.

Walter Pesavento was the workhorse of Ball State's pitching staff in the late 1930s. In 1937, he was the winning pitcher in a 7-6 victory over Indiana University. In 1938, he struck out 17 batters in a 10-2 victory over Taylor. In 1939, the left-hander won seven games, shutting out DePauw, 10-0, and Hanover, 1-0. It was said of Pesavento that when he had his control, he was invincible. Pesavento also lettered in football three years. As a fullback, he scored both Ball State touchdowns in a 12-0 victory over Hanover in 1938. Pesavento, who also played linebacker and punted, was named to the All-Secondary College team as a fullback by Indiana's sportswriters. In 1939, he was named to the All-State team.

Ball State's 1939 baseball team won the Indiana Intercollegiate Conference championship, the school's first league title in any sport, and recorded a 12-3 record. Members of the team were, from left to right, (front row) Kenneth Wasson, Robert Beall, Fred Bonebrake, Walter Pesavento, James Coughlin, John Eckley, Roscoe Bell, and Howard Locke; (back row) student manager Lloyd Biberstine, ? Hiatt, Gary Grabill, Alden Thompson, Mac McMarrell, ? Bailey, Maurice Applegate, Kermit Hummel, Walter Zumpe, Gabor Takats, and coach Billy Williams.

Coach Ray Louthen got his first Indiana Collegiate Conference baseball championship in 1961, when the Cardinals posted a 7-3 league record and finished 13-9 overall. Ball State then went to the small college NCAA Tournament at Greencastle, Indiana, where they defeated Ohio Wesleyan, 4-3, but lost to Southwestern (Tennessee), 5-3. Members of the team were, from left to right: (front row) John Bradley, Budge Hahn, Larry Dreasky, batboy Mike Louthen, Jerry Troxel, Ron Smith, and Phil Snodgress; (second row) Carl Harris, Dan Thurston, Dick Naylor, Don O'Connor, Myron Dickerson, Bob Jurgenson, Dean Campbell, and Bill Siderewicz; (third row) coach Ray Louthen, Roger Casterline, Tom Riutta, Mike Readnour, Bill Nixon, Doug Waldron, Barry Fritz, Tom Linville, and trainer Bud Miller; (back row) Jack Merritt, Arden Daugherty, Jim Wells, Jerry Hinkle, Dan Sullivan, student manager Meredith Rupe, and student manager Fred Reinke.

Ball State's 1962 baseball team repeated as Indiana Collegiate Conference champions, posting an 8-4 league mark and a 12-9 overall record. The Cardinals' most impressive victory of the season was a 2-1 verdict over Big Ten champion Illinois. Members of the team were, from left to right: (front row) Don Sherman, Tom Linville, Larry Jones, Phil Snodgress, Larry Dreasky, and Dan Thurston; (second row) Mike Readnour, Barry Fritz, Jerry Troxel, Dick Naylor, Bill Nixon, Doug Waldron, Tom Riutta, and Jerry Hinkle; (third row) Jack Merritt, Jim Wells, Ed Keil, coach Ray Louthen, assistant coach Chris Sweeney, Norm Kuhn, Colin Duffala, and Artie Daugherty; (back row) student manager Fred Reinke, Jim Chambers, Dan Dorman, Tom Lindenberg, Larry Moore, Ted Huber, Rollin Myers, student manager Gary Modlin, and student manager Meredith Rupe.

Ball State's 1965 team won the school's final Indiana Collegiate Conference baseball championship with a 9-3 league record and a 15-8-1 overall mark. The Cardinals also advanced to the NCAA District 4 Playoffs at Athens, Ohio, losing to Ohio State, 4-0, and Detroit, 4-3. During the regular season, the Cardinals defeated the Buckeyes once in a three-game series at Columbus. Also among Ball State's victories was a 3-1 verdict over Indiana University at Bloomington. Members of the team were, from left to right: (front row) Steve Paquin, Homer Jackson, Dave Langas, Bill Hajec, Al Genovese, Marv Rettenmund, and Steve Takats; (second row) Bob Rickel, Norm Troth, Dave Roberts, Wayne Schmitz, Freeman McGregor, Charles Nugent, and John Engle; (third row) coach Ray Louthen, Tom King, Jim Hughes, Larry Lewis, Pat Manley, Steve Davis, Frank Houk, and Larry Merica; (back row) student manager Ted Waltz, Ron Emrick, Charles Riddle, Steve Psikula, Bud Wetzel, Dave Amos, student manager Lloyd Fisher, and student manager Duane Foist.

Ball State's 1969 team achieved the greatest accomplishment in school history with two victories in the NCAA District 4 playoffs at Minneapolis. After the Cardinals lost to Southern Illinois, 15-6, on the first day, they defeated both Mid-American Conference champion Ohio University, 4-3, and Big Ten titlist Minnesota, 4-1, on the second day. A 4-3 loss to Southern Illinois the following day eliminated Ball State. Members of the team were, from left to right: (front row) Dave Torma, Pack Craig, Bill Brooks, Tom Pinkerton, Ron O'Neil, Jim Novar, and Rick Klemczewski; (second row) Al Bradford, Dave Wood, Steve Lane, John McCoy, Mike Pianowski, Dennis Barry, Lane Rhodes and Bob Coddington; (third row) coach Ray Louthen, assistant coach Bob Rickel, Tom Byers, Mike Hoffar, Al Christenson, Nino Muffoletto, student manager Mark Anderson, student manager Jeff Matanich, and trainer Ron Sendre; (back row) Dave Smith, Gary Gibboney, Frank Butiste, Larry Reveal, Lynn Jackson, Ron Campbell, Mark Savell, and Don Schmidt.

Members of Ball State's 1998 baseball team huddle in the middle of Ball Diamond after the Cardinals defeated Central Michigan to clinch the school's first Mid-American Conference championship in the sport. Chris Cabaj pitched a four-hit shutout as the Cardinals won the game by a 3-0 score. Two years earlier, Cabaj was the hard-luck loser in a 1-0 setback to Akron that prevented Ball State from advancing to the MAC Tournament.

Ball State's 1998 team provided the university with its first Mid-American Conference championship. The Cardinals edged Central Michigan for the title, which was decided by winning percentage. Ball State had a 23-8 record (.742), while the Chippewas finished 23-9 (.719). The Cardinals ranked 17th in the nation with a 4.14 earned run average, and with a 39-18 overall record, they finished 33rd in the country with a .684 winning percentage. Members of the team were, from left to right: (front row) student manager Dan Minix, graduate assistant coach Ken Jones, Justin Love, coach Rich Maloney, Brian Dorrmann, assistant coach John Lowery, and student assistant coach Jason Murray; (second row) Matt Deckman, Shayne Ridley, Tim Fitzharris, David Scheppele, Aaron Zehnal, Jeff Urban, Randy Farris, and graduate assistant trainer Brian Hatzel; (third row) student manager K.C. Hackman, Chad Wells, Nate Brown, Matt Speicher, Adam Sheefel, Jason Hickman, Jeremy Ridley, and student trainer John Flannel; (back row) Ryan Isaacs, Jamie Spottz, Ben Lassiter, Larry Bigbie, Chris Cabaj, Travis Minix, Jonathan Kessick, Matt Wood, and Jeff Randall.

Ball State won its second consecutive Mid-American Conference championship in 1999, recording a 25-6 league record and a 42-18 overall mark. Both victory totals are season highs for the Cardinals. Ball State led the conference with a .337 batting average, which ranked 14th in the country, and slammed 95 home runs, which was 16th in the nation. The Cardinals swept a three-game series with Michigan State, blasted Duke by a 9-0 score and edged Michigan, 6-5. Members of the team were, from left to right: (front row) Keith Nunley, Matt Deckman, Tim Fitzharris, Randy Farris, John Timm, David Scheppele, student manager Gregg Brody, and Eric Bava; (second row) Aaron Zehnal, Shad Turner, Nate Brown, Justin Crowell, Matt Speicher, Justin Wechsler, Brent Irwin, Adam Metzler, and Adam Sheefel; (third row) student trainer Jennifer Dial, graduate assistant trainer Brian Hatzel, Jeff Randall, assistant coach John Lowery, coach Rich Maloney, graduate assistant coach Chris Kessick, volunteer assistant coach Matt Husted, Ryan Isaacs, Travis Minix, and student trainer Matt Reedy; (back row) Shayne Ridley, Jason Hickman, Jonathan Kessick, Ben Lassiter, Larry Bigbie, Chris Cabaj, Jeremy Ridley, Matt Wood, Chad Wells, Doug Boone, and Scott French.

Ball State captured its third Mid-American Conference championship in three years, when the 2001 Cardinals finished atop the league with a 21-5 record. The Cardinals, who were 35-23 overall and ranked as high as 44th in the *Baseball America* magazine national poll, led the conference with a 4.72 earned run average and a .966 fielding percentage. Members of the team were, from left to right: (front row) student manager Josh Cooksey, James Nowicki, Jason Bucholtz, Keith Nunley, David Scheppele, Aaron Zehnal, Scott French, Eric Bava, and Matt Deckman ; (second row) Brian Lynch, John Pettibone, Kiel Holman, Paul Henry, Jimmy Long, Andrew Anderson, Dustin Ruhl, Justin Wechsler, Doug Boone, and Michael Hale; (third row) graduate assistant trainer Paul Herman, Adam Metzler, Matt Wood, Lorenzo Scott, graduate assistant coach Matt Husted, coach Rich Maloney, assistant coach John Lowery, volunteer assistant coach Mark Raikes, Brad Dorrmann, Patrick Lowrey, and James Campbell; (back row) Nate Brown, Bryan Bullington, Brian Harris, Troy Garrett, Rob Robbins, Brad Snyder, Kevin Sliwa, Jason Paul, Luke Hagerty, Brent Przybylski, and Mike Johnston.

Two

Diamonds in the Rough
From Wrought Iron Fences to a Brick Wall

Upon his first view of Ball State's baseball diamond north of University Avenue, coach Ray Louthen couldn't believe what he was seeing. In 1958, the diamond was covered by grass, with only gullies forming the base paths. The university's track ran through left field, with its concrete curb about 20 yards from the infield. Ground balls would reach left field and hit the curb and bounce over outfielders' heads. The portion of the track that served as the start for the 220-yard dash ran into right field.

There was no fence in left field, and in right field was a wrought iron fence that was only 250 feet from home plate down the foul line. Spikes protruded from the top of the fence. While Ball State players learned to avoid running into the fence, visiting players didn't. Crumpling upon impact with the fence was the fate of many opponents' outfielders, including one All-Big Ten center fielder from Indiana University who suffered a gash that spanned his entire chin. It was a frightening moment that stuck in Louthen's memory.

The pitcher's mound wasn't a mound. It was flat. Louthen measured the distance of the pitchers' rubber to home plate and found it to be 58 feet—2 1/2 feet shorter than the rules require. Areas of the field were a foot higher than other parts. There were no dugouts, only benches for the players. The gray color of the concrete stadium made it difficult for players to see the ball when it left a hitter's bat.

And then there was the tree that sat along the first-base line inside the stadium. President John R. Emens and others would sit in the stands shaded by the tree to escape the afternoon sun. Others in the stadium, however, couldn't see part of the diamond because of the tree. Louthen's first concern as coach was to improve the diamond—and the tree just had to go. Over President Emens' objections, Louthen had the tree chopped down. No longer could Emens sit in the shade and watch the Cardinals on the baseball diamond.

Other changes followed. The stadium was painted green. A tarpaulin was placed over the wrought iron fence. A snow fence was placed in left field, meeting the wrought iron fence in center field, about 375 feet from home plate. The new fence was hazardous, too. The Cardinals' Paul Snyder once caught a ball while tumbling over the fence. His pants caught on the fence and left him dangling headfirst while the opponents' runners circled the bases.

The field was leveled in some areas and sodded in others. A diamond was cut out of the grass. The pitching mound was raised, and the pitching rubber was moved to 60 feet 6 inches from home plate. Wooden walls were placed at the end of benches to simulate a sort of dugout.

It was a refurbishing long needed at the baseball field that had been used since 1928. Before then, the school had played on a field across University Avenue at approximately the present site of Burris School. At the field on the north side of University Avenue, a concrete stadium was constructed and dedicated in 1934. That's where the Cardinals' home baseball games were played through the 1970 season.

That was when Louthen became Ball State University's athletic director, ending his tenure as football and baseball coach for the Cardinals. Again he set out to improve the baseball facilities, but this time, he wanted a new ballpark placed on the southwest corner of Tillotson Avenue and McGalliard Road, near Ball State's new football field, which opened in 1967.

Louthen had played professional baseball with the coach at Ohio University, who allowed Ball State to copy that school's plans for its baseball stadium. Louthen proposed a design to have two diamonds back-to-back, one for the varsity team and another for the freshman squad. In the middle, he wanted a platform, so a coach could watch both teams practice at the same time. His plans didn't go quite the way Louthen wanted, though.

While the finishing touches were being made on the plans for the new ballparks, Louthen and his brother departed on a fishing trip to East Tawas, Michigan. After one afternoon on the lake, they went to a bar. Upon leaving the establishment, the two men—with three-day beards and beer on their breaths—immediately saw a Michigan state trooper with his foot propped up on the front of Louthen's car. Louthen looked at his brother, and his brother looked at him and said, "Wow, what did we do now?" The police officer asked, "Are you Mr. Ray Louthen?" After Louthen nodded nervously, the trooper, who had tracked down Louthen through his license plate number, informed him that he had an urgent message from the Ball State president. Louthen sighed and said to his brother, "Whew, I thought they had me."

Louthen called President Emens, who wanted to know whether the plans for the new baseball facilities could be changed, placing the two diamonds side by side as opposed to back-to-back, because the university wanted to use the area where the second diamond would have been for other activities. Still shaking from the sight of the trooper, a relieved Louthen quickly responded: "That would be fine. That's no problem, no problem."

Ball Diamond became Ball State's third baseball field in 1971, coach Bob Rickel's first season as coach. During Pat Quinn's coaching stint from 1983 through 1995, he concentrated on maintenance of the playing field, making Ball Diamond one of the most well-groomed diamonds in the Midwest. When Rich Maloney replaced Quinn as coach, he initiated plans for a renovation of the stadium. In his final year at Ball State before leaving for Michigan, a brick wall behind home plate was added.

Ball State's first baseman prepares to make a throw during action at the school's baseball diamond in 1930. The Cardinals posted a 5-9 record after beginning their season with two losses to Purdue and one to Indiana. Ivan Roetken was the top pitcher on the 1930 team.

A Ball State batter follows through on his swing during a 1931 game at the school's diamond. Despite a 4-8 record, the Cardinals managed a 12-3 victory at Purdue behind the pitching of Ivan Roetken. Outfielder John Brogneaux was captain of the 1931 team.

A cement stadium was dedicated at the Ball State baseball field in 1934. President John R. Emens and others enjoyed sitting in the shade of the tree that stood inside the stadium along the first base line. The tree was removed upon the insistence of Ray Louthen when he became the Cardinals' baseball coach for the 1959 season.

In 1941, the tree that stood inside Ball State's stadium cast a shadow over the home plate area. That season, the Cardinals accumulated a 7-8 record.

Ball Diamond, which opened in 1971, has a capacity of 1,700 fans. The dimensions are 330 feet down each foul line, 365 feet to the power alleys and 400 feet to center, with an eight-foot fence surrounding the field. In 2002, the fence that served as the backstop was replaced with a brick wall that stretched from dugout to dugout and a net that improved the vision of spectators.

Three

Making the Show
Cardinals in the Majors

Coach Ray Louthen once said that if a new game was introduced to a group of athletes, in 30 minutes Merv Rettenmund would have been the best player. That's the kind of talent Rettenmund displayed as a member of the Ball State baseball team in 1963 and 1964. Rettenmund also excelled in football as a Cardinal for three years and was drafted by the Dallas Cowboys before signing as a free agent with the Baltimore Orioles. And Rettenmund could have played basketball at Ball State, too, if he had wanted. Though stockily built, the 5-foot-10-inch Rettenmund could dunk a basketball. In fact, his contemporaries at Ball State say Rettenmund didn't think there was anything he couldn't do. "He had the mind to go with the talent," said Bob Rickel, one of his teammates.

Rettenmund often proved that. When he was at Ball State, gym classes participated in a game on the football field called flicker ball. A board with a 2 1/2-foot-square hole in it was placed on the crossbar of the goal posts at each end of the football practice field. By running with and passing the football, participants would try to get close enough to either throw the ball through the hole or hit the backboard. Points were awarded for both accomplishments. On one occasion, at the end of class, Rettenmund's team had the ball near midfield. He told Rickel: "Give me that ball. I'm going to throw it through that hole." That's exactly what he did — from nearly 50 yards away.

Rettenmund didn't limit such called shots to gym class either. One afternoon, Ball State was playing Valparaiso, which had a 6-foot-6-inch future pro baseball pitcher with a wicked fastball on the mound. After striking out his first time at bat, a disgruntled Rettenmund walked to the bench, plopped down, looked at Rickel and said, "I'm going to hit a home run the next time up to bat." Sure enough, Rettenmund did. And the right-handed slugger smashed another homer on his next trip to the plate.

On another day, Ball State entered the final inning of a home game tied with its opponent. Before strolling to the plate to lead off the bottom of the seventh, Rettenmund told Ball State batboy Mike Louthen, son of the Cardinals' coach, to put the bats away. "Sack 'em up, Mike," Rettenmund said. "This game's over." Without hesitation, Mike grabbed a bat bag and started putting bats into it. His dad, who was coaching at third base, glanced at the bench and saw what his son was doing. He went berserk and started running toward the Ball State bench, screaming, "Mike, what are you doing?" The coach didn't see Rettenmund hit the first pitch over the right field fence, across University Avenue and into the Ball Memorial Hospital parking lot. When Louthen turned around, he didn't know what had happened. Rettenmund just smiled at the coach as he rounded third.

An outfielder and catcher at Ball State, Rettenmund spent 13 seasons in the majors, playing for four teams. "Merv is without question the best baseball player who ever played at Ball State," said Ted Huber, his BSU teammate for two years.

Another candidate for "best player at Ball State" distinction would be Thomas Howard, who, like Rettenmund, played both baseball and football for Ball State. He became the university's first African-American quarterback in 1983 before talking coach Dwight Wallace into switching him to safety midway through his sophomore campaign. In Howard's second start at the new position, he was named Mid-American Conference Player of the Week. After that season, however, Howard, who entered the university on a football scholarship, left the gridiron program—despite the appeals of new BSU coach Paul Schudel, who had visions of his being an option quarterback—to concentrate on baseball. It turned out to be a wise choice because, the following summer, he made the USA Senior Team and then was drafted in the first round of the 1986 Major League Baseball draft by the San Diego Padres.

Those accomplishments probably sprung from his four-game performance at Florida State at the beginning of his sophomore campaign. Against the Seminoles, who were ranked fourth nationally at the time, Howard slammed five home runs, including a grand slam, as the Cardinals split the series against the perennial college baseball power. Howard was the target of abuse from the boisterous Florida State crowd throughout the series until his last at-bat, when he hit a home run, and the nearly 4,000 fans stood in unison and chanted, "Transfer, transfer, transfer," as the switch-hitting center fielder circled the bases. Howard, however, remained at Ball State until entering professional baseball and spending 11 seasons in the majors with six teams.

Ball State's third player to make the majors, right-handed pitcher Mike Roesler, played for the Reds in 1989, appearing in 17 games, and for the Pittsburgh Pirates the following season, pitching in five contests. Roesler was one of the most laid-back baseball players in Ball State history. Once at a critical moment in a hotly contested, crucial Mid-American Conference game, coach Pat Quinn went to the mound to talk to Roesler. When Quinn arrived, Roesler matter-of-factly asked, "What do you need?" Quinn didn't know how to answer that. The previous season, Roesler came up missing at a baseball practice. No one knew where he was. Later, it was discovered he had left early to play in an intramural rugby game.

Larry Bigbie became Ball State's second first-round draft pick when Baltimore selected him in 1999. He spent parts of both the 2001 and 2002 seasons on the Orioles' roster. Bigbie developed into a professional baseball player under Rich Maloney, who never had to worry about the left-handed hitting outfielder's dedication to the game. On March 27, 1999, Bigbie appeared too sick with the stomach flu to play against Wichita State on the Kansas school's campus. Bigbie, however, talked Maloney into allowing him to be the designated hitter on the condition that Bigbie return to the clubhouse to lie down between at-bats. In between naps, Bigbie smacked three hits in five at-bats, including a home run. On another occasion, after missing seven games with a severely sprained ankle, Bigbie was sent to the plate as a pinch-hitter with the bases loaded against Eastern Michigan. After he delivered a grand slam that helped Ball State to a victory, he could barely hobble around the bases.

Merv Rettenmund received All-Indiana Collegiate Conference first-team honors in both of his varsity seasons with Ball State. In 1964, he was selected as Ball State's Most Valuable Player after hitting .329 with five home runs and 23 runs-batted-in. Playing both outfield and catcher, he managed a .987 fielding percentage that season. As a sophomore, he hit .313 with seven homers and 18 RBI. Rettenmund signed a free-agent contract with the Baltimore Orioles before his senior season. In 1968, he was selected by The Sporting News as the Minor League Player of the Year after he hit .331 with 22 home runs for Rochester of the International League. He played in the majors from 1968 through 1980.

Thomas Howard finished his Ball State career with school records for at-bats (530), total bases (371), hits (189), games played (171), runs scored (164), runs-batted-in (152), home runs (43), game-winning RBI (20), slugging percentage (.700) and on-base percentage (.443). He was the Mid-American Conference Player of the Year in 1986 and was a two-time All-MAC first-team selection. After his junior season, Howard was drafted in the first round of the 1986 Major League Baseball draft by the San Diego Padres, who made him the 11th pick overall. He played in the majors from 1990 through 2000.

Left: Merv Rettenmund is greeted by Boog Powell after hitting a home run for Baltimore. As an Oriole, Rettenmund hit World Series homers in 1970 against Cincinnati and in 1971 versus Pittsburgh. He also homered for the Orioles against Oakland in the 1971 American League Championship Series.

Right: Merv Rettenmund receives a Ball State blazer from Don Lemish of the university's Alumni Office on July 19, 1970, in Chicago.

Opposite: Merv Rettenmund spent parts of 13 seasons as an outfielder in the majors, playing six seasons with the Baltimore Orioles, two with the Cincinnati Reds, two with the San Diego Padres and three with the California Angels. He finished his career with a .271 batting average, 66 home runs and 329 runs-batted-in in 1,023 games. In 1970, he led the World Series champion Orioles with a .322 batting average, slammed 18 home runs and drove in 58 runs. The following season, he ranked third in the American League with a .318 average while accumulating 11 homers and 75 RBI. He played in four League Championship Series and two World Series with Baltimore from 1968 through 1973. He also played with the World Series champion Reds in 1975 and helped the 1979 California Angels to the American League West title. In 13 World Series games, Rettenmund hit .200 with two home runs and six runs-batted-in. In 1977, Rettenmund set the Padres club record for pinch hits with 21, the eighth highest single-season total in Major League history. Rettenmund completed his 37th year in professional baseball in 2002 as hitting coach for the Detroit Tigers after spending the previous two years in the same capacity with the Atlanta Braves. He was the hitting coach for Oakland for 1989 and 1990 after three seasons as the A's roving hitting instructor. From 1983 through 1985, Rettenmund was hitting coach with the Texas Rangers. He was with California as bullpen coach in 1980, hitting coach in 1981 and minor league hitting instructor in 1982.

Thomas Howard joined the Cincinnati Reds in 1993 and remained with them through 1996. His best season was in 1995, when he hit .302 with 17 stolen bases—both career bests. That season, the switch-hitting outfielder also helped Cincinnati into the National League Championship Series against the Atlanta Braves. In the NLCS, Howard hit .250 with one run-batted-in. In 1997, he was a member of the Houston Astros, as they reached the postseason. Howard began his Major League career in 1990 with the Padres. He was traded to Cleveland early in the 1992 season and then to Cincinnati in the middle of the 1993 campaign. Howard played with Houston in 1997, the Los Angeles Dodgers in 1998, and the St. Louis Cardinals in 1999 and 2000. In 11 Major League seasons, Howard hit .264. In 1,015 games, he slammed 44 home runs and drove in 264 runs. He also collected 66 stolen bases. In 1996, while playing for the Reds, he ranked second in the National League with 10 triples. His other single-season highs were 122 games, 361 at-bats, 50 runs, 100 hits, 19 doubles, seven home runs and 42 runs-batted-in.

As a member of the Cleveland Indians in 1992, Thomas Howard batted .277 in 117 games. He also had a career-high 10 sacrifice bunts that season.

As a member of the USA Senior Team in 1985, Howard hit .358 with 11 home runs and 41 runs-batted-in. He also had 10 stolen bases. In the Simon Bolivar Games in Caracas, Venezuela, Howard batted .361 with four homers and nine RBI to help the USA Senior Team to a Bronze Medal.

Between 1982 and 1985, Mike Roesler started 50 games for Ball State, accumulating a 21-23 record. He was an All-Mid-American Conference second-team selection in 1985. The right-handed pitcher was a 17th-round draft pick of the Cincinnati Reds in 1985. Roesler spent six seasons in professional baseball. He appeared in 22 Major League games, playing with Cincinnati in 1989 and Pittsburgh in 1990. He managed a 1-1 record with a 3.60 earned run average, striking out 18 and walking 11 in 31 innings.

After becoming the Mid-American Conference Player of the Year for Ball State in 1999, Larry Bigbie was selected in the first round of the 1999 draft by the Baltimore Orioles, who made him the 21st overall pick. He made his Major League debut June 23, 2001, with the Orioles. The left-handed hitting outfielder finished the season with a .229 batting average, hitting two home runs and driving in 11. He also swiped four bases in 47 games. Bigbie spent most of the 2002 season with the Orioles' Triple-A team in Rochester before returning to the majors in September.

Four

Early Years
Coaches Sink, Williams, and Wann

In one of Gabor Takats' first games after switching from center field to catcher for his junior season, a batter lifted a pop up down the third base line near home plate. Takats threw off his mask, settled under the ball and yelled: "I've got it. I've got it." He caught the ball for the final out of the inning, rolled it toward the mound and headed toward the Ball State bench. But coach Paul B. "Billy" Williams, with his hands on his hips, was directly in the player's path. So Takats moved to his right, and Williams went the same direction. Takats moved to his left, and Williams again shifted into his path. When Takats got close to Williams, the coach said, "After this, it's 'I have it.'" Bill Reynolds, who played second base under Williams, said sometimes the coach would make players run laps around the field during practice for using such incorrect grammar. Williams would say, "This is a teachers college, and we are going to speak proper English."

Williams was an educator who became known as the father of Ball State's athletics program, serving as the school's director of athletics and head of the physical education department from 1921 through 1958. He launched Ball State's participation in football, tennis, cross country and golf plus also coached baseball and basketball at the school. He took over the baseball program in 1922 from professor Orville E. Sink, who coached the Hoosieroons' first three teams. Williams remained baseball coach through 1958, except for the 1927 season, when Norman "Happy" Wann took over the team while Williams was on leave.

A formal man, Williams rarely swore, although Takats might have heard the coach cuss on one occasion. That happened when Takats hit a line shot to right field, and the right fielder made a sensational catch. When Takats rounded first, he thought he heard Williams use profanity.

Williams was highly respected by his players, many of whom called him Mr. Williams. And Williams knew baseball. Fundamentally, he was a sound strategist. He played for one run. He would say: "We only have to win by one run. I don't care if the score is 15-0, you win by one run." As far as Williams was concerned, his players were at Ball State to get an education and not become professional baseball players. When a baseball player was enrolled in one of Williams' classes, the professor treated the player no differently than any other student. Although Williams possessed a strong desire to win, his main objective was to teach his young men what they needed to know as future teachers and coaches in the state of Indiana.

The education took many avenues. Takats, who was a soda jerk at the Pine Shelf—which, along with the Tally Ho, was a popular hangout for Ball State students—one time went with his boss, A.L. Sullivan, to a bank in downtown Muncie. Sullivan was taking a large amount of money and wanted somebody with him. On the return trip to campus, Sullivan and Takats stopped at a bar and drank a couple of beers until it was time for Takats to go to practice. "Billy and Sully didn't like one another," Takats says, "and Sully would just sort of get even with him through me." Upon Takats' arrival at the ball diamond, he put on his catching gear for batting practice. But he was having trouble catching the ball. Williams told him to take off the equipment and get up to bat. Takats couldn't hit the ball. Williams said, "Go on in," and sent

Takats to the locker room. The next day, at practice, Williams approached Takats and asked, "How are you feeling today?" Takats, who knew the coach had smelled beer on his breath the day before, answered, "Fine." Williams said, "OK." And nothing else was ever said about the incident.

A native of Sullivan County in Indiana, Williams graduated in 1911 from Prairie Creek High School, near Terre Haute, where he was nourished on a diet of Three-I League baseball in the days when that group of teams was nearly on a par with the American Association. Upon his graduation, he attended Indiana University for 12 weeks before teaching at three schools when a license wasn't required. He served four years in the Air Force and was commissioned as a bombing pilot in 1918. He was in New York ready to embark for France when the Armistice was signed to end World War I.

A 1919 graduate of Indiana State, his speed, aggressive hustle and cleverness made him one of the most outstanding basketball players the Sycamores have ever had. He also lettered in baseball at Indiana State. He received his master's degree from Columbia University and did graduate work at the University of Illinois and the University of Michigan. He completed requirements for a doctorate at Indiana University. Williams refereed basketball games for 30 years throughout Indiana, including at the state tournament in Indianapolis, while coaching the Ball State baseball teams.

"I have tried to advocate clean sportsmanship and clean living in the boys I've coached," Williams said upon his retirement from Ball State in 1958. He died in July 1973.

Before becoming Ball State's first baseball coach, Sink was a faculty member at Indiana State Normal School in Terre Haute. He moved to Muncie when Indiana State Normal School, Eastern Division, was established. A professor of Industrial Arts and Physical Education, Sink formed an Athletic Association in the fall of 1918. That spring, he started the baseball program. Glen Chenoweth was elected manager of the team by the student body and began seeking games with other schools in the state. While no results are known for that first campaign, Sink's 1920 team was 2-3 and his 1921 squad was 5-2. Sink was a member of Ball State's Athletic Committee from 1927 to 1939, serving as its chairman for three years.

Wann led Ball State to a 3-6 record in his only season as baseball coach in 1927. He also succeeded Williams as Ball State's football coach, guiding the Hoosieroons to records of 5-1-1 in 1926 and 5-2-1 in 1927.

Gabor Takats was a three-year regular in both baseball and football at Ball State from 1937 to 1940. On the diamond, he was the Cardinals' right fielder as a sophomore before becoming their starting catcher as a junior and senior. In 1939, Takats batted .369 and was the team's leader in home runs. Takats hit homers in both ends of a doubleheader with Hanover in 1939.

Coach Billy Williams demonstrates to members of the 1956 Ball State baseball team how to cross up the opponents by laying down a bunt. A sharp strategist, Williams played for one run at a time.

The institution that became known as Ball State fielded its first team in 1919 with Orville E. Sink as coach. The school was then known as Indiana State Normal School, Eastern Division, but referred to simply as Normal, thus the letter "N" on the uniforms. The team played local high schools and independent teams.

The 1920 baseball team recorded a 2-3 mark. Both of its victories came against Earlham. The Hoosieroons lost to Earlham, Indiana State and Rose Poly. Members of the team were, from left to right: (front row) Clifford French, Roscoe Baker, Aaron Belcher, ? Harding, Thomas Fields, and Arley Smail; (back row) Clifford Osbun, Don Knight, Ora Davis, ? Fadely, Haines Sleeth, coach Orville E. Sink, and John O'Hearn.

Billy Williams made his baseball coaching debut with the 1922 Normal baseball team. The squad posted a 6-5 record. The Hoosieroons scored 20 runs at Manchester but then allowed the same number at home versus Butler in their next game. The team defeated both Huntington and Danville twice, but dropped both of its games with rival Indiana State.

Opposite: Coach Billy Williams and his assistant, Bob Korsgaard, look out onto the Ball State baseball field in 1953. The Cardinals started the season with two victories but finished with a 5-12 record.

With Billy Williams on leave, Norman "Happy" Wann coached the 1927 Ball State team to a 3-6 record. The team started the season with Miami of Ohio, losing 6-1.

Virgil "Pop" Schooler became Ball State's first four-sport letterman, earning four monograms in basketball, three in football and two each in baseball and track from 1924 to 1928. He played outfield during his two years on the baseball team and served as the captain of the 1927 squad.

Carl Hinesley lettered three years as a pitcher for Ball State. In 1932, he held Franklin to five hits in a 17-4 Ball State victory and struck out 12 Valparaiso batters as the Cardinals won by a 12-4 score. In 1933, Hinesley pitched a six-hitter as Ball State handed DePauw a 10-1 loss and was the winning pitcher in a 14-5 Cardinal victory over Franklin.

A second baseman for Ball State from 1933 to 1935, Bill Reynolds posted the school's top batting average during his senior season. After college, he tried out with the Peoria Tractors of the Three-I League.

After retiring from Central Indiana Gas Company, Ball State baseball letterman Bill Reynolds began working with the kickers on the Cardinals' football team. Among those he coached was Brad Maynard, a two-time All-America punter who played with the New York Giants from 1997 to 2000 and the Chicago Bears in 2001 and 2002.

The 1935 Ball State baseball team enjoyed an 8-2 season. Members of the team were, from left to right: (front row) Marion Feasel, Eldon Bendit, Bill Reynolds, Donald Mohr, Fred Shearer, Herbert Edwards, Wallace Aylesworth, and Earl Manor; (back row) coach Billy Williams, Ernie Sutton, Harold Reasoner, Bill Stahl, Wendell Carr, Elmer Hampton, Lewis Henry, Burdette Hall, and Ray Katter.

As a second baseman, Max Rudicel on occasion teamed with his brother Rex to form Ball State's double- play combination during their three seasons on the team from 1936 to 1938.

Rex Rudicel played both shortstop and left field for Ball State from 1936 to 1938. He was the Cardinals' regular shortstop for two years and led the team in hitting in both 1936 and 1937. Rex was better known for his basketball skills. Nicknamed the Phantom Bantam, he was selected to the Little All-State team as a sophomore and to the Big All-State squad as a senior. He played for the Indianapolis entry in the National Basketball League, the forerunner of the National Basketball Association.

Curtis Rathburn rips the ball during a Ball State game in 1937. Rathburn, who lettered in 1937 and 1938, was described in the 1938 edition of the school's yearbook, the *Orient*, as "probably the club's smoothest player" and "a natural hitter with native ability above any other on the crew."

Ernie Sutton was the winningest pitcher in Ball State history at the time of his graduation in 1936. Sutton pitched Ball State to a 7-4 victory over Indiana University, allowing the Hoosiers just six hits—in both 1935 and 1936. As a senior, he posted a 7-3 record while fanning 61 batters. He also had 15 hits and scored four runs. As a sophomore, Sutton faced the minimum 27 batters in a nine-inning, 9-0 victory over Earlham. In the game, he allowed just two singles. Both of the players who reached base were picked off.

On May 19, 1941, Randolph Noel struck out 19 batters as Ball State defeated Manchester, 8-4. The strikeout total remains the school record more than six decades later.

Coach Billy Williams instructs his 1950 team on how to get a lead off first base.

After Ball State had no intercollegiate sports in 1944 because of World War II, coach Billy Williams had to rebuild the baseball team in 1945 without any veteran players, but the Cardinals enjoyed an 8-5-1 season. Members of the team were, from left to right: (front row) Robert Cruse, Loren Betz, and Victor Overman; (second row) Richard Doversberger, Charles Keller, Waldon Lewis, and Ray McShurley; (back row) coach Billy Williams, Richard Valandingham, Cyril Hall, Tom Craigmile, Michael Drake, Maurice Davis, and student manager Philip Trees.

With the return of servicemen in 1946, coach Billy Williams could find more players for the baseball team. The 1946 Cardinals posted a 5-7 record. Members of the team were, from left to right: (front row) Louis Abbott, Charles Posey, Orville Wiebusch, James Gardner, William Tate, and Paul Elliott; (second row) student manager Wayne Johnson, Robert Rhoda, Raymond Gilbert, Robert McKenzie, William Bender, James Roush, Richard Brainerd, Jack Lewis, and assistant coach Walter Gray; (back row) William Albrecht, Arthur Rehbein, James Eichhorn, Maurice Davis, coach Billy Williams, Ray Munger, Walter Molinder, Charles Marcus, and Harry Allison.

Ball State's Bill Loose awaits a throw as a DePauw runner slides into third base during a 1952 game. The 1952 Cardinals defeated DePauw twice during the season en route to a 7-7 mark.

Ball State's returning players for 1948 were, from left to right, Charles Marcus, Raymond Gilbert, William Bender, Charles Keller, James Roush, Harry Allison, and Don Havens. The 1948 Cardinals finished with a 5-7-1 record.

Members of Ball State's 1952 team await their turn at bat.

Senior members of the 1957 Ball State baseball team were, from left to right, Don Lockwood, Jerry Sprunger, Wally Smith, Jerry Banker, Wayne Van Sickle, Richard Meister, Terrance Craig, Charles Sanburn, and student manager Allen Souder. The leading hitter on the 1957 team was first baseman Wayne Campbell, who hit .400. Sanburn, the Cardinals' third baseman, hit .386, and left fielder Earl Van Sickle batted .344 with three home runs and 13 runs-batted-in. The team posted a 5-7 record and had six games rained out.

Five

The Louthen Era
Flint Helps Ignite the Program

Ray Louthen coached high school baseball and football in Flint, Michigan, before he joined the Ball State staff in 1958 as the head man on the diamond and an assistant on the gridiron. So it was logical that Louthen recruited players from the Flint area, many of whom he had coached in high school, to play both sports. There were 31 such athletes, most of whom were two-sport participants. Some baseball players, such as future Major Leaguer Merv Rettenmund, really didn't want to play football, but many football players, such as George Hathaway, wanted to play baseball in order to avoid spring practice.

Rettenmund, who played for Louthen as a Little Leaguer in Flint, was a member of an American Legion team from Flint, Michigan, that produced five future Ball State athletes. After watching the team play in a tournament in Princeton, Indiana, Louthen signed Rettenmund, his cousin Marv, Bill Hajec, Dave Roberts and Wayne Schmitz. All but Schmitz played both baseball and football at Ball State for Louthen, who became the Cardinals' head football coach in 1962.

The baseball program really took off with the influx of the Flint players. But there was some resentment from the players from Indiana high schools who thought Louthen favored the Flint players. Indiana high school coaches even spread the word that if a player wasn't from Flint, he wouldn't play for Louthen. The truth was Louthen recruited only sure bets from Flint—players who he was convinced could play at the collegiate level. And, obviously, the presence of only 31 players, three of whom didn't finish their careers at Ball State, proves there was room for BSU players on the diamond other than Flint products. But when the Cardinals' lineup was announced before a game, it was strange to hear that four or five players were from Flint, Michigan, Louthen admitted.

Louthen was a demanding coach, but players wanted to play for him. He was a motivator who made players believe that they could reach a higher level. Behind his back, Louthen was often referred to as the "Old Man," a term of affection. The players didn't always like him, but they always respected him. "You got from him what you gave," said Ted Huber, who lettered for three years in both baseball and football for Louthen in the early 1960s. "If you put it on the line for him, then he put it on the line for you, and if you didn't, he wouldn't. It was as simple as that. And, if you didn't, you didn't stick around long."

Huber got a taste of Louthen's discipline on at least one occasion. Louthen had an outfielders drill during which he would hit fly balls to the players, each of whom would have to catch five in a row before they could leave practice for the day. It was more for conditioning than skill development, because the fly balls would increasingly require running longer distances to catch. One afternoon, Huber was the last player on the field and had caught four consecutive fly balls. Louthen must have been ready to call it a day, so he hit the next ball directly at Huber. But Huber, who played catcher more than outfield, dropped the ball. Irritated with himself, Huber threw the ball into Christy Woods, which sat beyond the third-base line. Louthen beckoned Huber to his side and sternly told him, "Go get the ball." Huber hunted and hunted for the ball but couldn't find it. Then student manager Meredith Rupe arrived to help Huber look. But still no luck. Finally, Rupe found a worn-out baseball that had obviously been exposed to the elements for a long time. Huber was tired of looking, so he and Rupe took the ball to the Old Man. "It's the wrong ball," Louthen grumbled. "Go find the ball you threw in there." Huber returned to the woods to continue his search. A while later, Rupe approached Huber with a ball, which the exhausted player knew wasn't the one he had thrown into the woods. Huber, who surmised that the ball probably was given to the student manager by Louthen, took the ball to the coach, who just said: "Thank you. You can go in now."

Rupe was a straight arrow-type of student manager who was in charge of handing out Chiclets to the players. Louthen would tell Rupe how many pieces of the gum he could give each player—usually two or three—before a game, and the student manager would never exceed the allotted number no matter the amount of pressure he would receive. Players would whine, "Come on, Meredith, give us some more Chiclets." Uncompromisingly, Rupe would reply, "Coach said three Chiclets, and that's what you get." Then Rupe would always return the boxes with Chiclets remaining in them to Louthen—even a box that had just one piece of the gum left inside. He wouldn't even consider chewing that last Chiclet himself. After graduation, Rupe became a minister.

Others weren't so pious. Pitcher Bill Nixon, a hard-throwing right-hander who wasn't shy about throwing at batters, had arm problems as a senior and lost his velocity. But he knew how to pitch and continued to win games. One afternoon, however, catcher Ted Huber became irritated with the lollipops Nixon was throwing to the plate and walked toward the mound. Huber got to within about 10 feet of Nixon before the senior pitcher looked at the sophomore catcher and said amid an expletive-laced tirade, "You take one more step, and I'm going to throw the ball right between your eyes." Forty years later, Huber reminded Nixon of the episode, and Nixon said, "I remember, and I would have hit you." Huber responded, "Yeah, I know you would have, and it probably would have been the hardest you threw all day."

Louthen served as Ball State's baseball coach from 1959 to 1970, leading the Cardinals to a 158-127-1 record and three Indiana Collegiate Conference baseball titles. He also was the BSU football coach from 1962 to 1967, accumulating a 37-13-3 mark and directing his teams to four consecutive ICC championships. In 1970, Louthen became Ball State's athletics director and remained in that position until his retirement in 1986.

Opposite: Ray Louthen accumulated a record of 158-127-1 as Ball State's baseball coach from 1959 to 1970. He was the Indiana Collegiate Conference Coach of the Year four times and led the Cardinals to three ICC titles.

B
BALL STATE

Outfielder Nat Pittman led the 1959 Ball State baseball team with a .379 batting average while collecting four home runs and 15 runs-batted-in. He was named to the All-Indiana Collegiate Conference first team in 1960.

Pitcher Carl Harris recorded a 5-3 record with a 1.99 earned run average in 1961, earning All-Indiana Collegiate Conference second-team honors. The previous spring, he broke a bone above his ankle in a sliding drill and missed the entire season.

In addition to lettering two years in baseball for the Cardinals, Merv Rettenmund was a three-year monogram winner in football as a running back. His career rushing average of 7.6 yards per attempt remains a school record. During Rettenmund's Ball State career, his cousin, Marv, started at quarterback for the football team and at second base for the baseball team. Marv earned honorable mention on the All-Indiana Collegiate Conference baseball team in 1964.

Bill Nixon (left) and Dean Campbell (right) receive some hitting instruction from coach Ray Louthen. Campbell was the Indiana Collegiate Conference Player of the Year in 1961 and was a two-time All-ICC first team selection. In 1960, Campbell batted .388 with one home run and 22 runs-batted-in plus posted a 6-1 record with a 1.86 earned run average. Nixon was a three-time All-ICC pick, making the first team in 1960 and the second team the next two years. In 1960, he managed a 1.85 ERA—the fourth best mark in Ball State history—en route to a 4-3 mark. His career 2.85 ERA also ranks fourth on the Cardinals' all-time list.

Mike Henderson was the All-Indiana Collegiate Conference second-team first baseman in 1960, when he batted .261. As a member of the Ball State basketball team in 1959-60, he averaged 15.3 points a game.

Centerfielder John Bradley made the NCAA All-Mideast third team in 1961, when he hit .266. The three-year regular for Ball State hit .304 during his sophomore campaign in 1959.

Tom Riutta is greeted by his teammates after hitting a home run at Ball State's baseball diamond. The 6-foot, 205-pound first baseman was the Cardinals' most valuable player and an Indiana Collegiate Conference first-team choice in 1961 after he batted .293 with a team-high five home runs and 21 runs-batted-in. In a double-header with DePauw in 1961, Riutta had six hits in eight at-bats. That same season, he hit two home runs against Wabash. Riutta was elected captain of the 1962 Cardinals.

In 1962, Mike Readnour batted .451, the second-highest single-season mark in Ball State history. In addition to being the Indiana Collegiate Conference Player of the Year that season, the outfielder was elected Ball State's most valuable player. He also was an All-Indiana Collegiate Conference first-team choice after making the second team in 1961. Readnour was the most valuable player for Ball State's 1960-61 basketball team, making him one of only two Cardinals to earn the honor on both the diamond and court. Larry Bullington was the other.

Doug Waldron was the All-Indiana Conference first-team third baseman in both 1961 and 1962. As a junior, he batted .291 with three home runs and a team-high 22 runs-batted-in. The next spring, he hit .271 while leading the Cardinals with five home runs and 18 RBI.

Jim Wells was selected the most valuable player of the 1963 Ball State baseball team. The second baseman hit .372 with four home runs and 15 runs-batted-in that season and had a .910 fielding percentage. He signed a contract with the Milwaukee Braves and played two years in the minors. He became an assistant coach at Ball State in 1973.

Merv Rettenmund and Wayne Schmitz were two of coach Ray Louthen's top recruits out of Flint, Mich. Rettenmund holds the Ball State record for home runs per game with an average of 0.28, having hit 12 in 43 games in 1962 and 1963. Schmitz's 2.11 career earned run average ranks second on Ball State's all-time list. In 1965, Schmitz was 7-1 with a 2.30 ERA en route to making the All-Indiana Collegiate Conference first team. In 1964, he was 5-2 with a 1.34 ERA, and in 1963, he managed a 6-6 record with a 2.64 ERA.

Ted Huber, who both caught and played the outfield for Ball State, made the 1964 All-Indiana Collegiate Conference first team in 1964, when he hit three home runs and drove in 16 runs while compiling a .986 fielding percentage. The RBI total ranked second on the team, and his five doubles tied for the team high. Huber also was named BSU's honorary captain for the 1964 season. As a junior, Huber hit .299 and led the team with four doubles. In addition, Huber was a three-year football letterman for the Cardinals as a guard and offensive end. He was elected most valuable player as a senior in 1963, when he was named to the All-ICC second team.

First baseman Charles Nugent batted .299 with five home runs and 28 runs-batted-in for the 1965 Ball State baseball team, earning a spot on the All-Indiana Collegiate Conference first team.

Bill Hajec, a three-year letterman as a running back for the football team, earned two monograms as a pitcher for the baseball squad at Ball State. On the diamond, his best season was in 1965, when he was selected to the NCAA All-Mideast Second Team and the All-Indiana Collegiate Conference first team. That spring, he posted an 8-5 record and a 1.22 earned run average. That ERA ranks as the second-best single-season mark in Ball State history.

Ball State's first two-time most valuable player in baseball was Homer Jackson, who won the award in both 1965 and 1966. He was a three-year regular, starting at shortstop his first two seasons before moving to second base. He made the All-Indiana Collegiate Conference first team in 1966 and shared the ICC most valuable player award with his teammate Frank Houk that year. Jackson was named to the NCAA All-District Four first team as a senior after earning third-team honors the previous season. Jackson hit .395 with five home runs and 15 runs-batted-in in 1965 and .333 with three homers and 15 RBI in 1966. The New York Mets drafted Jackson in 1966, and he played one year in the minor leagues.

Ed Sherry became the first Ball State athlete in any sport to earn All-America honors in the university division, when he made the third team in 1967. An outfielder and pitcher, Sherry batted .455—the school's single-season record—and posted a 7-1 mound mark with a 3.38 earned run average. Also following the 1967 season, Sherry was placed on the NCAA All-District Four and All-Indiana Collegiate Conference first teams plus was selected as both the ICC's and Ball State's most valuable player. In addition to leading the 1967 Cardinals in hitting and victories, Sherry was first on the team with 35 hits, five doubles, four home runs and 17 runs-batted-in. As a pitcher, he topped the team with 58 1/3 innings and 46 strikeouts. The following season, Sherry made the All-ICC second team and was named the Cardinals' honorary captain. He batted .301 and led the team with 30 runs scored, six doubles and 21 walks.

In 1968, Jim Roudebush earned All-America second-team recognition, the highest award for a Ball State baseball player up to that time. Also a first-team NCAA District Four choice in 1968, he was selected as the most valuable player of the Indiana Collegiate Conference that year and made the All-ICC first team as both a junior and senior. Roudebush was also Ball State's most valuable player in 1968, when the outfielder batted .398 with five home runs and 37 runs-batted-in while fielding .979. As a junior, he hit .380 with three homers and 11 RBI. His .360 career batting average ranks sixth in Ball State history. During Ball State's 12-game winning streak in 1968, which included five victories over Big Ten teams, Roudebush drove in 22 runs, including the winning tally on five occasions. Roudebush climaxed his career with a defensive gem on the 1968 season's final day, falling over the left-field fence while robbing a St. Joseph's College hitter of a grand slam to preserve Ball State's 4-3 victory. Roudebush spent one year in the Chicago White Sox organization before playing four seasons with the Kokomo Highlanders, a semiprofessional baseball team.

Frank Houk shared the Indiana Collegiate Conference Most Valuable Player Award with his teammate Homer Jackson in 1966 and was named to the NCAA District Four third team in 1967. After moving from outfield before his junior season, Houk was a two-year starter at shortstop, earning All-ICC first-team selection both springs. Houk led Ball State in hitting as a junior with a .350 batting average. He was named honorary captain after the 1967 campaign. Also a three-year letterman in football, the quarterback earned most-valuable-player honors at the 1965 Grantland Rice Bowl, completing 12 of 15 passes for 155 yards and two touchdowns as Ball State and Tennessee State battled to a 14-14 tie. Houk played two seasons in the Kansas City Athletics organization.

John McCoy started three seasons for Ball State's baseball team—at second base as a sophomore and at shortstop the next two years. He was named to the All-Mideast second team in 1969, after he led the Cardinals with a .344 batting average, 32 hits, 24 runs scored, nine doubles, four home runs and nine stolen bases. As a junior, he received honorable mention on the All-Indiana Collegiate Conference team after batting .301 and stealing 12 bases. During the 1966-67 season, McCoy also was a member of the Ball State wrestling team, finishing second in the ICC in the 152-pound weight class.

Mike Pianowski was the All-Indiana Collegiate Conference first baseman in both 1967 and 1968. As a junior in 1968, he batted .283 with five home runs and 19 runs-batted-in. Pianowski compiled a career .985 fielding percentage, which ties for the 14th best in Ball State history.

Larry Reveal's 1968 season ranks as the most dominating pitching campaign in Ball State history. The strong-armed right-hander, who specialized in a sharp-breaking over-hand curve, posted a 9-2 record with a school-record earned run average of 0.98. He didn't surrender a home run until the final game of the season. Of the 47 hits he allowed, all but six were singles. Reveal pitched two-hit shutouts against both Purdue and Northwestern and blanked Butler on three hits—all on the road. He completed seven of his nine starts. The only two he didn't finish were against Indiana State, when he was relieved in the 10th inning, and versus DePauw, when he left after pitching shutout ball for six innings and with Ball State owning a sizeable lead. Reveal's losses were to Michigan State, which scored the only two runs of the game in the final inning, and to Indiana State in extra innings.

Coach Ray Louthen poses with Jim Novar, who was the captain of the 1970 Ball State baseball team. A two-year letterman as an outfielder and third baseman in baseball, Novar also received three letters in football for the Cardinals.

Dennis Barry was elected most valuable player of the 1970 Ball State baseball team after leading the team with a .330 batting average and 22 runs-batted-in. Barry was a starter at first base as a sophomore and junior before moving to the outfield as a senior. He was the seventh-round selection of the California Angels in the 1972 Major League Baseball draft.

Six

The Rickel Era
Hello, MAC

When Ray Louthen became athletic director at Ball State in 1970, he handpicked Bob Rickel to succeed him as coach. With the blessing of Dr. John Reno, then the chairman of the division of physical education and athletics, Louthen interviewed no one else for the position before naming his former third baseman baseball coach. He ignored the fact that Rickel's coaching experience was limited to one year as BSU's freshman coach, two as a junior high coach, one as a graduate assistant for Louthen, and one as the junior varsity baseball coach at Blackford High School. Louthen wanted someone who would carry on the program that he had built, and Rickel was the logical choice. He was loyal to Louthen and Ball State, but his inexperience resulted in his moving the program along slowly—too slowly for what was ahead for the Cardinals.

"It was a challenge, but what a great opportunity," Rickel said. "A lot of it has to do with being in the right place at the right time. Ray looked at me as someone who was young, loved the game and wanted to excel and become a quality coach plus someone who loved Ball State and wanted to be a part of college baseball. To this day, I know I was one of the luckiest people I know. It was the opportunity of a lifetime, and I had to take it even though I knew I was inexperienced."

Having withdrawn from the Indiana Collegiate Conference in 1968, Ball State now had a schedule that no longer featured such schools as St. Joseph's, Valparaiso and DePauw, who the Cardinals left behind when they gained major college status for athletics. Those top rivals for the BSU baseball teams were being replaced by more schools from the Big Ten and Mid-American Conference. In Rickel's first season as coach, Ball State became a member of the Conference of Midwestern Universities along with Indiana State, Illinois State, Northern Illinois and Southern Illinois. Ball State finished at the bottom of the baseball standings both seasons of the league's existence.

Then in 1974, Ball State joined the Mid-American Conference, and the competition became even stronger. MAC members Ohio University, Eastern Michigan, Western Michigan, Kent State, Bowling Green, Miami University and Toledo boasted some of the most respected baseball programs in the Midwest. While Rickel was still settling in as a collegiate baseball coach, he was faced with challenges for which Ball State's baseball teams weren't prepared. The result was ninth- and eighth-place MAC finishes the first two years in the powerful league.

But the Cardinals' prospects improved dramatically in 1976 primarily because of three players from the Flint, Michigan, area, where Louthen had found much of his top talent when he raised the Ball State program to the top of the Indiana Collegiate Conference 15 years earlier. With Louthen's assistance, Rickel landed left-handed pitcher Tom Sharon of Flint Southwestern in 1974, outfielder Demetrius Sanders of Flint Northwestern in 1975, and infielder Greg Dikos of Swartz Creek—a Flint suburb—in 1976. The result was one of Ball State's most successful baseball seasons in its history. "We just had great chemistry," Rickel says, "and things just fell into place."

What might have helped was the weather. It was a warm spring, and when the Cardinals returned from their Florida trip, they never had to return to indoor practices. Ball State also lost only two games to the weather that spring—a doubleheader with Indiana State. Ball State won 22 of its first 25 games in 1976 en route to a 34-14 record. The 34 victories were a school record that wasn't matched until 10 years later and wasn't surpassed until 21 years later, when coach Rich Maloney's 1997 squad posted a 40-19 mark. The .708 winning percentage of the 1976 Cardinals was the best since the .714 mark managed by coach Billy Williams' 10-4 squad in 1947 and had not been bettered through the 2002 campaign. Ball State swept doubleheaders with Purdue and Indiana and split a twin bill with Notre Dame. Six losses in their first eight MAC games, however, doomed the Cardinals to a fifth-place finish in the league, as they finished with a 10-10 conference record. "That shows the caliber of the other teams in the MAC," Rickel said.

Sanders became Ball State's first All-MAC choice that season, batting .348 and setting school records with 37 stolen bases in 40 attempts and 55 runs scored. "He was a human BB," Rickel said of the center fielder. Jeff Mathew, Rick Morrison, Rich Canada and Bob Brannock also hit over .300. "Jeff Mathew was a young man who would bust his tail to improve," Rickel said. "He was a walk-on who just kept getting better."

Sharon was the ace of the pitching staff, managing a 9-3 record with two saves and a 3.33 earned run average. On occasion, Sharon would start the opener of a four-game weekend series and then serve as a closer for the finale. "He could pitch every day," Rickel says. "He had a rubber arm. He wanted to throw. He could throw strikes, and he was smart. He just knew how to pitch." While Morrison came to the Ball State baseball team from the football program, Stu Moyer joined the Cardinals on the diamond after completing his season as a wrestler. His addition solidified the mound corps that also included Ray Lyttle, Dave Van De Wielle and Randy Myers.

While Ball State never again under Rickel reached the pinnacle of success attained in 1976, there were success stories, such as Ralph Hartnagel. The first two times Hartnagel tried out, Rickel cut him. After failing to make the BSU team as a catcher first and then as a third baseman, Hartnagel tried out as a shortstop and made the team. "He had too much giddyup not to keep," Rickel says. When Ball State's starting shortstop was injured, Hartnagel stroked three hits in his first game and never was out of the lineup the rest of his career. "Coaches from other teams would say, 'Boy, I wish I had a player like that Hartnagel kid,'" Rickel said.

Rickel resigned as Ball State's baseball coach after 12 seasons in 1982, having been overwhelmed by the strain of coaching, teaching and recruiting, and disappointed with the progress of the program. "I have one regret, and it was not using Ray Louthen as a mentor or using his expertise," he said.

Opposite: Bob Rickel was the only Ball State baseball player to become head coach of the Cardinals' diamond program. He was the Cardinals' regular third baseman for coach Ray Louthen from 1963 to 1965 and served two years as his graduate assistant coach. Rickel succeeded Louthen in 1971 and remained as Ball State's coach through the 1982 campaign. In 1976, Rickel led Ball State to a 34-14 overall record and a fifth-place finish in the Mid-American Conference. In his 12 years as coach, Rickel compiled a 209-217-2 record as the Cardinals strengthened their schedules.

B
Cardinals

Demetrius Sanders is the greatest base stealer in Ball State history, swiping 107 bases from 1975 to 1978. When he graduated, he also owned the school career record for runs scored with 137. In 1976, he set BSU single-season records with 56 hits, 55 runs scored and 37 stolen bases. That year, the center fielder became the school's first baseball player named to the All-Mid-American Conference first team. He received All-MAC honorable mention in 1975.

Top Left: Steve Lane, who played both infield and outfield, was the most valuable player for Ball State's 1971 team after hitting .318. He also scored 20 runs, collected 35 hits and managed five stolen bases.

Top Right: Catcher Tom Blacketer was the only Ball State player named to the all-league team of the Conference of Midwestern Universities during its two years of existence, earning the distinction in 1972. Blacketer moved into the Cardinals' starting lineup in the ninth game of his freshman campaign in 1971 and remained BSU's regular catcher for the remainder of his four seasons.

Right: Larry Bullington was named the most valuable player of Ball State's 1972 baseball team after leading the team with a .363 batting average and 23 runs-batted-in. The infielder, who didn't play baseball as a senior, accumulated a .307 career average. His son, Bryan, pitched for Ball State for three years before becoming the overall No. 1 selection in the 2002 Major League Baseball draft.

Mike Hoffar, who lettered in baseball for Ball State from 1969 to 1971, enjoyed his best season as a Cardinal in 1969, when he managed a 5-2 record with a 2.66 earned run average. He posted a 6-7 mound mark during his last two seasons before signing a free-agent contract with the Kansas City Royals in 1971.

Outfielder Don Presser batted .303 as a junior and .310 as a senior for Ball State before signing a professional contract with the Pittsburgh Pirates in 1974.

Greg Minegar, who played two years at West Palm Beach Junior College, accumulated a .326 career batting average for Ball State in 1973 and 1974. The right fielder was named most valuable player for the Cardinals in 1973 after he led the team with a .345 average.

Tom Sharon threw two shutouts during the week of April 11-18, as Ball State defeated both Central Michigan and Anderson by 3-0 scores. The left-handed pitcher allowed just two hits to the Chippewas, who entered the week as the Mid-American Conference's top-hitting team, and limited Anderson to five hits. Sharon, who was selected to the Mid-American Conference second team in both 1976 and 1977, holds the Ball State career record for complete games with 26 and is second in wins with 28. He shared BSU's most-valuable-player award with Stan Neuenschwander in 1977.

Coach Bob Rickel's 1976 baseball team posted a 34-14 record and finished fifth in the Mid-American Conference. Members of the team were, from left to right: (front row) Dave Van De Wielle, Stan Neuenschwander, Rich Canada, Demetrius Sanders, Kevin Patterson, Dave Hinke, Jeff Mathew, Jim Stanley, Randy Myers, Tom Sharon, Art Yaroch and Bob Brannock; (second row) student managers Ron Buck, Bob Divine and Earl Schenck, assistant coach Tom Knowles, Jeff Eader, Dale Strzelecki, Mike McWhorter, Ray Lyttle, Charles DeMarco, Greg Dyer, Richard Utley, Jay Brehm and Greg Dikos; (back row) coach Bob Rickel, Corey Goers, Bill Stahl, Dave Rouch, Bud Brown, Al Rzepka, Rick Morrison, Jim Letzel, Robert Wittkamper, Stewart Fox, Steve Bellamy, and trainers Larry Pappas and Ron Sendre.

Jim Stonecipher was a slick-fielding first baseman for Ball State in 1974 and 1975, earning most-valuable-player honors for the Cardinals as a senior, primarily because of his .984 fielding percentage. He hit .239 with three home runs and 21 runs-batted-in. He received honorable mention on the 1975 All-Mid-American Conference team.

Third baseman Bob Brannock earned All-Mid-American Conference second-team selection in 1976 after receiving honorable mention in 1975. He was Ball State's most valuable player in 1976 after hitting .307 with eight home runs and 44 runs-batted-in. He also led the team with five triples, six sacrifice flies and 86 total bases. When he graduated, he owned or shared seven school records.

Outfielder Dave Hinke led Ball State in hitting in 1975 with a .347 batting average, which ranked sixth in the Mid-American Conference. He was named to the All-Mid-American Conference second team that season.

Dave Van De Wielle became the first Ball State baseball player to win a Mid-American Conference weekly award, when he was selected MAC pitcher of the week for April 25 to May 1, 1976. The right-hander threw two shutouts, blanking Notre Dame on three hits in a 9-0 rout and Western Michigan on four hits in a 7-0 victory. That gave Van De Wielle three straight shutouts, because he had whitewashed Kent State on three hits in a 3-0 verdict April 23. Van De Wielle received honorable mention on the 1976 All-MAC team.

Two of coach Bob Rickel's best hitters and students in the late 1970s were Greg Dikos and Mike Sullivan. Dikos, a three-year regular at third base, was both an All-Mid-American Conference and Academic All-MAC first-team selection in 1979 plus made the All-Mideast Region team. He also received All-MAC honorable mention in 1976 and a MAC Scholar-Athlete Award in 1979. Sullivan was co-MVP of the baseball team and earned Academic All-MAC first-team selection in 1980. He was co-captain of the 1979 Cardinals and a tri-captain the next year. The third baseman batted .407 as a senior and .322 as a junior.

Greg Dikos' son, Greg Jr., holds the baseball that his dad hit for his record-setting 24th career home run May 8, 1979. Sally Dikos joins her husband and son. Dikos, who finished his career with 28 homers, ranked ninth in the nation in 1979 with 12 round-trippers. Also that year, he ranked third in the Mid-American Conference and 18th in the country with 42 runs-batted-in and placed 14th in the league with a .358 batting average.

Randy Myers pitched a no-hitter versus St. Joseph's on May 11, 1977, facing the minimum 21 batters in the seven-inning game. One St. Joe batter walked in the fourth, and another reached on an error in the seventh, but both were erased on double plays. Myers posted a 4-2 record with a 2.83 earned run average in 1977 and finished his career with a 10-4 mark. A math and computer science major, Myers earned Academic All-Mid-American Conference first-team honors in 1977 and honorable mention in 1976.

Catcher Stan Neuenschwander was named to the Academic All-America third team in 1977, when the physical education and journalism major owned a 3.61 grade-point average on Ball State's 4.0 scale. That season, he was also NCAA All-Mideast Region third team and All-Mid-American Conference second team. Neuenschwander was Academic All-MAC for three consecutive years. He set BSU records with 10 home runs in 1977 and 23 career homers. In 1977, he hit .344 and broke Ball State single-season marks with 88 runs-batted-in and 193 total bases.

After being cut twice by coach Bob Rickel, Ralph Hartnagel finally made the Ball State team in 1980 and batted at least .300 each season while serving as the Cardinals' regular shortstop all three campaigns. As a senior, he batted .308 and managed a .906 fielding percentage. The previous campaign, he hit .304 and led Ball State with nine doubles while fielding .945. In his first season on the BSU team, Hartnagel batted .300.

Rick Morrison was a four-year regular for Ball State's baseball team and a three-year starter for the Cardinals' football team. On the diamond, Morrison, who played second base and the outfield, posted a career .286 batting average with the help of a .333 mark during his freshman campaign and a .336 effort as a junior. In a double-header with Indiana State on May 4, 1976, he had two inside-the-park home runs, one a grand slam. As a split end in football, Morrison earned All-America honorable mention in 1977 after ranking fifth in the nation with 59 receptions.

Right-handed pitcher Butch Wickensheimer was an All-Mid-American Conference second-team choice in 1979 after he posted a 6-3 record with a 3.51 earned run average. That season, he pitched a one-hitter against Notre Dame, as the Cardinals nipped the Irish by a 2-0 score. He finished his Ball State career second in appearances, third in wins, fourth in innings pitched and eighth in strikeouts. He was the 18th-round selection of the Los Angeles Dodgers in the 1979 Major League Baseball draft.

First baseman Ted Weigel made the All-Mideast Region second team and the All-Mid-American Conference first team in 1979, when he hit .362 with seven home runs and 31 runs-batted-in. He served as a tri-captain for the 1980 Ball State baseball team. That spring, he received Academic All-America honorable mention.

Catcher Scott Rafferty receives his plaque as a 1980 Academic All-American from Garnis Hagen (left) of U.S. Tobacco Company in Kansas City, Missouri. Assisting in the ceremony is Brigham Young's Dave Schultes (right), president of the College Sports Information Directors of America. Rafferty, Ball State's first University Division Academic All-American, ranked sixth in the Mid-American Conference with a .392 batting average in 1980 and owned a 3.73 grade-point average on the university's 4.0 scale as a business management major.

Don DeWitt shut out Mid-American Conference champion Central Michigan on three hits April 25, 1980, as the Cardinals managed a 1-0 victory. The right-handed hurler, who possessed a 90-mph fast ball, was an All-Mid-American Conference second-team choice at the end of that season. The 6-foot-3-inch DeWitt, who first attended Cal Poly Pomona on a basketball scholarship, spent just two seasons with the Cardinals, posting a 3-2 mound mark, before signing with the New York Yankees.

Tom Pougnet ranked seventh in the Mid-American Conference in hitting in 1981 with a .382 average. He also slugged four homers and drove in 21 runs that season. The third baseman, who hit .300 the previous season, was an Academic All-MAC choice in 1981 before receiving honorable mention in 1982.

A bloop single in the first inning was the only hit Rob Robbins allowed in a 3-0 victory over Miami University on April 19, 1980. Robbins, who was 2-2 with a 4.97 earned run average in 1980, was an Academic All-Mid-American Conference choice that season. Robbins signed with the St. Louis Cardinals in 1981, following two brothers into professional baseball. His son, Rob, was a member of Ball State's baseball team in 2000 and 2001 and lettered for the Cardinals' basketball team.

Seven

THE QUINN ERA
BIG BATS AND BRAWLS

Oohs and aahs first oozed from the mouths of fans at Ball Diamond on May 13, 1986, when Mark Davis drilled an outside pitch from an Ohio University hurler over the right field wall and the ball took one hop before hitting a passing car—driven by Ball State Athletics Director Don Purvis' wife, Pat—on Tillotson Avenue. The oohs and aahs intensified later in the game when Dru Kosco drilled a home run over Tillotson and into the football parking lot. But the oohs and aahs reached a crescendo in the second game of the doubleheader when Thomas Howard blasted a homer over the flagpole in center field that bounced against a bus in the intersection of Tillotson and McGalliard avenues. "I'm not sure we're ever again going to see three guys at Ball State who could prolifically hit the ball the way those guys did," coach Pat Quinn said.

With Howard establishing a Mid-American Conference record with 23 round-trippers and Davis and Kosco adding 15 each, the 1986 Ball State baseball team established 10 of Ball State's single-season offensive records. Howard and Davis both batted over .400 as other outstanding hitters, such as Paul Burghardt, Tom Kilgore, Ty Allen and Chuck Laumann, were completely overshadowed by the big three. Howard, though, could overshadow everyone by himself. Such a day occurred at Chicago State when he hit for the cycle and went six for six with two home runs and a two-run triple in a 16-12 victory. Howard also starred in Ball State's 8-4 verdict over the Louisville Redbirds, the AAA affiliate of the St. Louis Cardinals. Howard slammed a two-run homer and an RBI single in the exhibition game.

Nicknamed "Tank" since he was a plump child, Howard was also instrumental in another highlight of Quinn's 13 seasons as Ball State's coach—the Cardinals' southern trip in 1985. Howard ripped eight homers and drove in 23 runs in 12 games as Ball State recorded an 8-4 record, which was highlighted by a four-game split with Florida State and victories over Georgia and Kentucky. In the Cardinals' 2-1 decision over Georgia, Howard singled in BSU's first run and then stole second, third and home to give Ball State its second run. Defensively, he reached above the left field wall to rob a Bulldog hitter of a grand slam, caught a ball thigh high as he crossed the left field foul line and leaped over the fence before he could stop, and later threw out a runner at the plate. After the game was halted by rain in the seventh inning, winning pitcher Mike Roesler was upset the game didn't go the complete nine innings. "Doggone it," he said as he sat in the dugout. "I had these guys eating out of my hand." His teammates, especially Howard, looked at him in amazement.

Quinn's teams were known for hitting with things other than bats. Such players as Tom Kilgore never shied away from a fight, many times defending his teammates. One such case was at The Citadel, when that school's fans berated Howard with racial slurs. Late in the game, Howard streaked into third base, where Quinn was coaching. Howard said to Quinn, "Coach, I don't know how much more of this I can put up with." Quinn said: "Tank, you just have to take it. You just have to behave yourself. You just have to suck it up." Then Quinn saw Howard's eyes grow wide. The coach turned around and saw Kilgore in the stands, fighting with a group of cadets who had been verbally attacking Howard. Another time, at the University of Toledo, a fan began heckling Ball State pitcher Tom Dilley, who started toward the man upon his sticking his head in the Ball State dugout. Kilgore stopped Dilley, but when the fan continued his barrage when he reached the BSU bullpen, Kilgore took off toward him. This time, Howard grabbed Kilgore. Then the fan, after climbing over the fence, called Howard a racial name. Howard jumped the fence and grabbed the man once he caught him in the middle of the street. Quinn got to Howard before he could do any damage to the man, who was committed to a mental institution the following day after Toledo's coach reported him to police. The next day, during pregame practice, two policemen approached Quinn at the batting cage for information on the incident. While talking to the officers, Quinn looked toward the outfield where Howard had been. He wasn't there. Thinking he was going to be arrested, Howard was hiding in the woods behind the center field fence.

Quinn was a battler, too, never shying away from voicing his disagreement with an umpire's call. But in so doing, he sometimes received responses that left him speechless. Once Laumann crushed the ball to right field, where it hit the foul pole for an apparent home run. The first base umpire, however, threw his arms in the air and motioned that the ball was foul. Quinn rushed the umpire and asked why he ruled the ball foul. The umpire calmly asked, "Well, why do you think it's called a foul pole?" The home plate umpire overruled the decision. Another time, a Ball State batter stroked the ball down the left field line, sending chalk flying. Quinn again charged the umpire, questioning his ruling. The umpire said, "It hit on the foul side of the chalk line." That time the decision stood.

In such situations, Quinn often was ejected from the game after getting his say. In fact, once he got the heave-ho for arguing for a Ball State opponent. It happened in a game with Taylor University, after a batter for the church-affiliated college hit a ball off his foot. Nobody moved, as the ball lay on the ground. The umpires didn't make any call, so finally the Ball State third baseman retrieved the baseball and threw to first base, where the umpire called the batter out. Quinn went onto the field and told the umpires: "Everybody in the ballpark knows that was a foul ball except you three guys. Do we have three blind mice out here working?" Quinn was quickly excused from the premises.

But the craziest moment during Quinn's career might have been Laumann's imitation of Babe Ruth. During a rain delay during a game with Central Michigan, Laumann stuffed towels under his shirt and impersonated the Bambino hitting a home run and trotting around the bases, looking just like the Yankee legend in old game footage.

Quinn's coaching career came to an end in 1995, when he was named assistant athletic director for Ball State.

Coach Pat Quinn lies flat on the ground to make sure that Shannon McCormick slides into third base during a game with Bowling Green on April 12, 1985. McCormick, who played second and third base for the Cardinals, was an All-Mid-American Conference second-team choice in 1985. Quinn guided Ball State to fourth place in the Mid-American Conference standings three times from 1983 to 1995, compiling an overall record of 323-389-6.

Chuck Laumann played in high school for coach Pat Quinn, who recruited him to the University of Cincinnati. When Quinn left Cincinnati to take over the Ball State baseball program, Laumann transferred into the Cardinals' program. In 1986, Laumann, who played first base and outfield at Ball State, earned Academic All-Mid-American Conference selection and received honorable mention on the All-MAC team after hitting .305.

As Scott Murr lays down a bunt, Ball State photographer John Huffer finds himself on the other side of the camera. Huffer shot many of the pictures in this book. Murr, who earned All-Mid-American Conference honorable mention as a catcher for three straight seasons, shares the Ball State record for career sacrifice bunts with Ron Murphy. Both had 17 between 1990 and 1993.

In a doubleheader with Huntington College on May 16, 1983, Kent Lynch tripled in three consecutive at-bats. The second baseman led the Mid-American Conference with eight triples in both 1981 and 1983, ranking among the top 10 in the nation both seasons. Nationally, he tied for eighth in 1981—when Ball State led the country with 31 triples—and finished seventh in 1983. The eight triples and his 20 career three-baggers are Ball State records. Lynch was BSU's most valuable player in 1981, when he hit .351, and earned All-MAC second-team honors in 1983, when he batted .338.

After ranking second in the Mid-American Conference to teammate Kent Lynch with five triples in 1983, Gary Brown topped the league with seven in 1984. Brown ranks second in career triples at Ball State with 16. The outfielder was selected to the All-Mid-American Conference first team in 1984 and the second team in 1983. Brown hit .342 with six homers, 33 runs-batted-in and 10 stolen bases in 1983.

First baseman Scott Goss was Ball State's most valuable player in both 1983 and 1984. He was an All-Mid-American Conference second-team pick in 1984, when he led the Cardinals with a .390 batting average, 45 runs-batted-in and a school-record 64 hits. Goss ranked third in the league in RBI and fifth in batting. In 1983, he ranked second in the conference in home runs with 10 and third in RBI with a school-record 48. Goss finished his BSU career No. 1 in hits with 180, total bases with 302 and RBI with 139.

Ron Schrock, who tied for eighth in the country with nine saves in 1985, owns the Ball State career record for saves with 24 and shares the single-season mark for relief appearances with 29 in 1985. The right-hander's 11 saves in 1984 rank second on Ball State's single-season list and his nine the following year tie for third.

Coach Pat Quinn was always ready to go to any heights to promote Ball State's baseball program in an effort to help the Cardinals climb to the top of the Mid-American Conference. In 1984 for a publicity photo, the university's sports information office talked Quinn into sitting on top of the batting cage while his team looked up at him.

As a senior in 1986, Thomas Howard led the Mid-American Conference in hitting with a .448 batting average—the third highest mark in Ball State history—in runs scored with 70 and in home runs with 23. The home run total, which remains a BSU record, was a new MAC standard, as were his 94 hits and 188 total bases. He ranked 11th in the nation in batting and 16th in home runs. Howard had set MAC records in 1985 with 17 home runs and 69 runs-batted-in. Howard also spent two seasons on the Ball State football team, lettering as a sophomore when he played in eight games. After switching from quarterback, he started the final five games of the 1984 season at safety. He led the team in interceptions with three and finished 10th in tackles with 42. He also blocked two kicks.

Between transferring from Florida State and signing with the Seattle Mariners after being selected in the 13th round of the 1986 Major League Baseball draft, Dru Kosco played just one season at Ball State. The outfielder made the All-Mid-American Conference second team after batting .343 with 15 home runs and 54 runs-batted-in. He tied for third in the league in homers and ranked fifth in RBI. He also tied for third in doubles with 15 and sixth in runs scored with 54. Kosco's father, Andy, played 10 seasons in the majors.

Mark Davis, who played first and third base during his Ball State career from 1984 to 1987, was named to the All-Mideast Region first team after his senior season, joining nine Big Ten players on the 10-man squad. He was an All-Mid-American Conference second-team choice his final two seasons after receiving honorable mention as a sophomore.

Mark Davis completed his Ball State career in 1987 as the Mid-American Conference all-time leader in hits with 259, doubles with 65, runs-batted-in with 190 and total bases with 443. His marks for hits, doubles and total bases remain the best in Cardinals baseball history. As a senior, Davis led the league in hitting with a .426 average and doubles with a school-record 21. He tied for second in the conference with 52 runs-batted-in and shared fourth with 10 home runs. As a junior, Davis ranked fourth in the conference with a .401 batting average plus led the league in doubles and ranked third in RBI, runs scored and home runs.

Mike Shebek tossed two one-hit shutouts against Miami University in 1986 en route to a 9-5 record and a 3.68 earned run average. The right-handed pitcher tied for first in the Mid-American Conference in wins, and his ERA ranked sixth. In addition, his 70 strikeouts ranked third. He was selected to the All-Mid-American Conference second team that spring. He was drafted in the 38th round of the 1987 Major League Baseball draft by the Baltimore Orioles but returned for his senior season. His eight career shutouts are a Ball State record, and his 257 career strikeouts rank second on the BSU all-time list.

Paul Burghardt, who pitched and played first base for Ball State in 1986 and 1987, received honorable mention on the All-Mid-American Conference team both seasons. In 1986, he batted .344 with seven home runs and 36 runs-batted-in. As a pitcher, the left-hander posted an 8-3 record with one save. The following campaign, he posted a 5-4 record with a 4.01 earned run average.

Second baseman Ty Allen attempts to turn a double play in a game at Ball Diamond. Allen, the son of former Major Leaguer Bernie Allen, played for Ball State from 1985 to 1988. He received honorable mention on the 1987 All-Mid-American Conference team after hitting .294 with six home runs and 32 runs-batted-in. In 1986, he batted .311.

Tom Kilgore rounds third base in a Mid-American Conference game with Miami University on April 10, 1984, at Ball Diamond. The catcher made the all-league second team in 1986 after batting .322 and driving in 49 runs—the fourth-highest total on the team. He led the Cardinals in both sacrifice bunts with six and sacrifice flies with five. Kilgore was All-MAC honorable mention in 1985 and 1987.

Carl Siegrist slides back into first base safely on a pick-off attempt by Miami University in 1987 at Ball Diamond. Siegrist, an outfielder who began his Ball State career as a catcher, set a Mid-American Conference record in 1987 with 42 stolen bases. He also batted .330 with two home runs and 20 runs-batted-in that season to make the All-MAC first team. In 1986, Siegrist hit .273 with 27 stolen bases in 30 attempts.

Ball State's 1986 baseball team ranked third in the Mid-American Conference in batting with a .326 average. The Cardinals claimed fifth in the league standings with a 17-15 mark. Members of the team were, from left to right: (front row) Mike Hepler, Tom Klaer, Tom Kilgore, Tom Blosser, Lex Hunter, Mike Overmyer, Shane Hall, Dave Harris, Paul Whitesell, Chuck Laumann, Dave Minnich, and Randy Dudeck; (second row) Alan Condon, Dru Kosco, Mark Davis, Wayne Throgmorton, Jeff Hartnagel, Scott McKinney, Paul Burghardt, Tom Sefton, Tom Dilley, Jim Dunham, Shenan Murphy, Carl Siegrist, and Mike Newell; (back row) trainer Thanh Nguyen, trainer Andy Bennett, Bill Setser, Mike Taylor, Ty Allen, Mike Hoffman, Mike Shebek, Jason Uyeda, Dave Childers, Thomas Howard, assistant coach Bob Lowden, and coach Pat Quinn.

Denny Rieman, a four-year regular at second base, flips the baseball to shortstop Mike Newell for a force-out on April 22, 1987, at Ball Diamond. Rieman, in 1990, was the male winner of the Mid-American Conference's Bob James Award for academics, character, leadership, and citizenship. Rieman, a pre-medicine major, owned a 3.94 grade-point average on Ball State's 4.0 scale. He earned Academic All-America second-team honors in 1990, Academic All-MAC selection three times and Academic All-District Five honors twice. He received honorable mention on the All-MAC team in 1988.

Third baseman Mike Hepler prepares to tag out a Central Michigan runner April 19, 1988, at Ball Diamond. Hepler was named to the All-Mid-American Conference first team in 1987, when he ranked third in the league with a .364 batting average. In 1988, he was on the All-MAC second team after tying for second in the conference in doubles with 12. Hepler was named the MAC Hitter of the Week for May 8-14, 1989, when he had 13 hits in 22 at-bats, scored four runs, drove in six runs and managed a .667 on-base percentage.

Tom Dilley pitched a no-hitter versus Ferris State in 1988, as the Cardinals posted a 6-0 victory. The right-handed pitcher was named Ball State's most valuable pitcher that season and received honorable mention on the 1987 Academic All-Mid-American Conference team.

Pitcher Dave Childers was named to the All-Mid-American Conference first team in 1989 after earning honorable mention in 1986 and 1988. He was named to the Academic All-District Five team in 1989. A marketing major, he graduated cum laude from the Honors College with a 3.62 grade-point average on Ball State's 4.0 scale. Childers received honorable mention on the All-MAC team in 1988.

Dave Brust was selected as Ball State's most valuable player both seasons he played for the Cardinals after transferring from Monroe Community College. As a senior in 1989, the catcher made the All-Mid-American Conference second team after ranking third in the league with 14 home runs and 11th with a .342 batting average. In 1988, he led Ball State with nine homers and 37 runs-batted-in. He was selected MAC Hitter of the Week for April 11-17, 1989. He had four hits in Ball State's 15-7 victory at Kentucky in 1988. He played second base in a four-game series with Kent State due to an injury to Denny Rieman and handled 20 chances without an error. Brust signed a free-agent contract with the Atlanta Braves in 1989.

Pitcher Bob Couet earned honorable mention All-Mid-American Conference honors in 1990, when he posted a 5-7 record with a 4.45 earned run average. The right-handed hurler was Ball State's most valuable pitcher that season. He started 14 games, completing six of them and recording two shutouts.

Curt Conley needed only 60 pitches as he tossed a no-hitter versus Miami University on May 5, 1992, as Ball State managed a 3-0 victory. The next day, the left-hander threw 1 1/3 innings in relief and got the win in the Cardinals' 8-3 verdict over Miami. Conley was named Ball State's most valuable pitcher three straight years. In 1993, he was named to the All-Mid-American Conference second team after he recorded a 9-4 mark with a 4.36 earned run average. He also made the 1993 All-MAC Tournament team. He was chosen in the 26th round of the 1993 Major League Baseball draft by the Colorado Rockies.

Switch-hitting Darrell Betts didn't need to take any swings in Ball State's game with Butler on March 29, 1995. In that contest, the lead-off hitter walked four times, setting a school record. Betts was Ball State's most valuable player in 1995, when he led the team with 31 runs scored and 40 walks. The shortstop also led the team with 131 assists and managed a .931 fielding percentage to earn best-defensive-player honors. Betts, the cousin of former major leaguer Daryl Boston, was the 26th-round selection of the St. Louis Cardinals in the 1996 Major League Baseball draft.

Shortstop Curtis Greene and pitcher Eric Jones join former Ball State Athletics Director Don Purvis at midcourt between halves of a Ball State basketball game, during which the two Cardinals were honored for being named Academic All-America third-team selections in 1992. Greene, an exercise science major, owned a 3.39 grade-point average on Ball State's 4.0 scale, while Jones, a pre-med major, had a 3.80. Eric, the son of Indiana's 1963 Mr. Basketball, Rick Jones, went on to become a doctor.

Curtis Greene turns one of the 108 double plays he completed during his career from 1989 to 1992. A record when he graduated, the double-play total now ranks fifth in Ball State history. Greene was All-Mid-American Conference honorable mention in 1990 and 1992 and was chosen as the Cardinals' most valuable player in 1991. He was an Academic All-MAC first-team selection in 1991 and 1992.

Corey White earned All-Mid-American Conference honorable mention in 1993 when he batted .321 while playing the infield and recorded a league-high eight saves after taking over as Ball State's closer. In 1994, when he batted .333, he tied a school record with four stolen bases in an 8-4 victory at Georgia Southern. He led the team that season with 14 stolen bases. He also topped the Cardinals with 56 hits and ranked second with 12 doubles. He also was No. 1 on the Ball State team in assists with 100. White singled in his first collegiate at-bat—versus West Florida on March 2, 1991. He began a triple play at Kent State on April 27, 1991.

Shortstop Michael Thompson awaits the Ball State catcher's throw as an opponent attempts to steal second base during a game at Ball Diamond. Thompson, himself, was an effective base-stealer for the Cardinals, swiping 24 bases as a senior in 1993 to lead the Mid-American Conference and 56 during his four-year career. The cousin of Ball State star Thomas Howard, Thompson hit .331 as a senior, when he earned All-MAC honorable mention and was named Ball State's most valuable player, and .312 as a junior. He was named to the 1993 All-MAC Tournament Team.

Brad Stewart slides safely into first base against Bowling Green in action at Ball Diamond. When Stewart completed his career at Ball State in 1990, he ranked fourth on the university's list for games played with 197. He was also fifth with 520 at-bats, tied for fifth with 30 doubles, eighth in hits with 153 and tied for third in sacrifice bunts with 10. The outfielder received honorable mention on the 1988 All-Mid-American Conference team.

Derrick Westfield gets the safe signal from the umpire after stealing second base against Kent State. Westfield, who transferred to Ball State in 1988 when Wichita State dropped its football program, played both football and baseball for the Cardinals, gaining All-Mid-American Conference honorable mention in both sports. The outfielder was Ball State's most valuable player in baseball in 1990, when he hit .309 with eight home runs and 40 runs-batted-in. The 6-foot-2-inch, 220-pound defensive end played 22 games for Ball State's football team, starting 10.

Kenny Reed made the All-Mid-American Conference first team in 1993 after hitting .321 for the second straight season, leading the league with 15 home runs and tying for second with 43 runs-batted-in. The catcher and designated hitter was the MAC Co-Hitter of the Week for April 5-11, 1993, when he was seven-for-15 with seven RBI. Reed was an All-MAC second-team choice in 1992, when he tied for third in the conference with a team-high eight homers. He tied for fourth in the league with 40 RBI, which also topped the Cardinals. Reed, who was drafted out of high school by the Atlanta Braves, was selected in the 18th round of the 1993 Major League Baseball draft by the Baltimore Orioles.

Ryan Read might have left Ball State as the most bruised Cardinal baseball player in history. He set a school record by being hit by pitches 24 times in 1995 and 40 times in his final two seasons. On April 29, 1993, against Ohio University, he set a school record by being hit three times in a game. In one stretch during that season, he was plunked by pitches in five straight games and in another span of seven games, he was hit by a pitch in six of the contests. Fittingly, on the last day of his collegiate career, he was hit by a pitch in both ends of a doubleheader. In 1994, the second baseman was named honorable mention on the All-Mid-American Conference team after hitting .321 and recording a .474 on-base percentage.

Toby Ricard only hit 18 home runs in his Ball State career and just six as a senior in 1995. But in a doubleheader at Central Michigan on April 22 of that year, Ricard hit a homer in the first game and then slammed two in the second contest. In the two games, he was four for five with six runs-batted-in. In 1994, he set a Ball State record with eight RBI in a 17-9 victory at Indianapolis on March 15. He again had two home runs in that contest. The game before, he also had two homers at Augusta. In his first collegiate plate appearance, he tripled off the right field wall against Vanderbilt in 1992.

In addition to being selected as Ball State's most valuable player in 1994, Brian Houdeshell was named to both the All-Mid-American Conference second team and the Academic All-MAC first team for the second time. The first baseman hit .355 with eight home runs and 48 runs-batted-in that season and finished his career with a .300 batting average. In 1993, he was voted to the Academic All-District Five team. In Ball State's first doubleheader sweep of Central Michigan, Houdeshell had five hits, scored four runs and drove in six April 16, 1993. He was also an All-MAC second-team choice in 1992.

Dan Lehrman is greeted by coach Pat Quinn on March 24, 1994, as the Ball State outfielder rounds third after hitting one of his 35 career home runs as a Cardinal. That total ranks fourth on the BSU career list. Lehrman was a two-time Academic All-American, earning first-team honors in 1993 and second-team selection in 1994. He was also a two-time Academic All-District pick and a three-year Academic All-Mid-American Conference choice. Lehrman was named to the All-MAC first team in both 1992 and 1993, and received All-MAC honorable mention in 1991 and 1994. He was named to the All-Mideast Region second team in 1993.

On March 26, 1991, one week after suffering a broken jaw when hit in the face by a throw on a pick-off attempt at Indiana State, Dan Lehrman, wearing a protective mask, tied an NCAA record when he hit two home runs in an inning versus IUPUI—one batting left-handed and one batting right-handed. With Ball State trailing by an 8-3 score in the sixth inning of the seven-inning game, Lehrman entered the game as a pinch-hitter and slammed a two-run homer. He came to bat a second time in the 10-run inning and smacked a three-run round-tripper to lift Ball State to a 13-8 victory.

Eight

The Maloney Era

Feeling a Draft

Rich Maloney's impact on Ball State's baseball program quickly became apparent after he was named the Cardinals' coach in 1995. His immediate influence was apparent from his first team winning 32 games, the combined victory total for the Cardinals the previous two seasons. But what Maloney inserted into the Ball State program went far beyond wins and losses. That was exemplified at the end of his first campaign in Muncie. In the final game of the 1996 regular season, the Cardinals were denied a Mid-American Conference Tournament berth when they suffered a 1-0 loss on Ball Diamond. The wailing that came from the dugout after that game was heart-wrenching. Maloney and assistant coach John Lowery were both crying, and so were the players. It was like they had just learned of the death of a loved one. When Bob Moore, assistant director of athletics communications, put his arm around Maloney to try to console him, the coach said, "This is about the toughest loss I've ever experienced."

Although Ball State had several other hard-to-accept setbacks during Maloney's seven-year reign as coach, the Cardinals never again failed to make the MAC Tournament. In fact, Ball State became the dominant team in the league from 1998 through 2001, winning three league championships and finishing first in the West Division all four years. In Maloney's second season at Ball State, the Cardinals set a school record with 40 victories. Two years later, they passed that mark with 42. Ball State's sad days during the Maloney era were usually reserved for the MAC Tournament, which was the biggest prize because winning it meant a trip to the NCAA Tournament. An incredible string of misfortunes—including injuries to top players—prevented the Cardinals from achieving that goal. But the always-positive Maloney consistently reminded people that Ball State remained the envy of the league because of its incredible regular-season success.

Most of the tears during Maloney's years were reserved for happy days, including the day the coach stood next to the fence at Madison High School and watched Bryan Bullington warm up for a game. Maloney's wife, Kelle, approached him and asked why he had tears in his eyes. He responded, "I'm watching the best high school pitcher in the nation, and he's coming to Ball State." Bullington, three years later, became the overall No. 1 selection in the 2002 Major League Baseball draft. The 6-foot-5-inch right-hander could have gone to any school in Indiana. Some recruited him for both baseball and basketball. He was named Indiana's Mr. Baseball after leading his team to the state championship. He played basketball for his father, Larry, a former most valuable player both on the diamond and court at Ball State. Bryan ranked seventh in Indiana high school basketball in scoring as a senior with an average of 23.6 points a game. He had a desire to play both sports at Ball State, but with Maloney's encouragement, decided to concentrate solely on baseball.

Bullington also could have gone directly into professional baseball out of high school. He had been drafted after graduation—the 37th-round pick of the Kansas City Royals. But that wasn't the situation with most of the 22 players who were drafted—some more than once—during Maloney's years at Ball State. Such players as outfielder Larry Bigbie, a first-round selection, and, even more so, pitchers Jeff Urban and Luke Hagerty—both of whom were supplemental draft picks between the first and second rounds—developed under the tutelage of Maloney and Lowery. More and more high school players with professional aspirations flocked to the Cardinals' program, contributing to the vision Maloney had of building a strong baseball tradition at the school.

In Maloney's first years at Ball State, he used big hitters to win games. During the 1999 season, for example, the Cardinals—featuring four double-digit home run hitters in Bigbie, Matt Wood and identical twins Jeremy and Shayne Ridley, blasted a conference-record 95 homers in 60 games and ranked sixth in the country with a .566 slugging percentage. At times that spring, Ball State would obliterate opposing pitching staffs. In a 23-7 victory over Purdue, Bigbie, Jeremy Ridley and Wood hit back-to-back-to-back home runs. In a four-game sweep of Eastern Michigan at Ball Diamond, the Cardinals scored 58 runs, crossing home plate at least 10 times in every contest.

Maloney loved playing at Ball Diamond. When the wind was blowing toward the outfield fences—which was the vast majority of the time—his eyes would sparkle like a child on Christmas morning. "The Great Cardinal is looking out for us today," he would say. And when on the road, if the wind was blowing out, he'd smile and announce to the team, "It's just like being at home." And Maloney felt at home at Ball Diamond, where the Cardinals had a .753 winning percentage during his time as BSU's coach.

In many ways, Maloney was just as successful off the field. He was an effective fund-raiser, bolstering the Ball State baseball budget and improving Ball Diamond with the help of contributions from drafted players who remembered the Cardinals' program when they received signing bonuses. "In talks to our team," Bullington said, "he focused on giving back not to just baseball but to things that you believe in, whether it's your church, your hometown, your high school or the Ball State baseball program—things you have a positive experience with and enjoy." Maloney's door was always open to players to talk about any concerns they had, whether they were baseball-related or not. He also preached the importance of academics and reached one of his primary goals in his final campaign at Ball State, when the team had an accumulative 3.0 grade-point average on the university's 4.0 scale.

What Maloney did best, however, was make his players believe in Ball State baseball and convince them they could play at a higher level. Bullington was one of them. After the right-hander suffered a 3-2 defeat at Kentucky to drop his record to 0-2 early in his junior campaign, Maloney sat with him in the dugout at the Wildcats' field the next day and told his star pitcher he needed to start throwing a slider along with his fast ball and curve ball. "I definitely thanked him for that," said Bullington, who went on to win 10 straight games and finish with an 11-3 record. Bullington was a big part of Maloney's change of philosophy halfway through his stint at Ball State. After his power-hitting lineups in the late 1990s couldn't produce a MAC Tournament title and a berth in the National Collegiate Athletic Association Tournament, he placed greater emphasis on pitching depth at the dawning of a new millennium.

But Maloney never realized the great dreams he had for the Ball State program, including NCAA Regional berths and the complete renovation of Ball Diamond. He had another dream that much preceded his years with the Cardinals. A native of Detroit, who graduated from high school in nearby Roseville, Maloney had long dreamed of being a member of the baseball program at the University of Michigan. He wanted to go there as a player, but the Wolverines didn't recruit him. So he went to Western Michigan, where he earned All-America third-team selection before becoming a 13th-round draft pick of the Atlanta Braves. After six seasons in the minor leagues, his dream of playing in the majors didn't evolve, but after seven years at Ball State, his dream of going to Michigan did. In 2002, he was named baseball coach of the Wolverines and was replaced by Greg Beals, a nine-year assistant at Kent State, the school that had eliminated Ball State from the MAC tourney each of the previous two years.

Coach Rich Maloney pays a visit to the mound to talk to pitcher Justin Wechsler during a game at Ball Diamond. Maloney guided the Cardinals to a seven-year record of 256-144-1 for a .640 winning percentage from 1996 to 2002. In Mid-American Conference games, Maloney's BSU teams were 141-60 for a .701 winning percentage. After his first team tied for fifth in the league, he led the Cardinals to four West Division titles and three MAC Championships. Maloney was named MAC Coach of the Year in 1998 and 2001.

Coach Rich Maloney was all smiles at a press conference announcing the selection of Jon Kessick (left) and Larry Bigbie (right) by the Baltimore Orioles in the 1999 Major League Baseball draft. Bigbie went in the first round with the 21st pick overall, and Kessick was a third-round choice. They were two of the five Cardinals drafted in 1999.

Side-winding right-handed pitcher Nick Witte led the Mid-American Conference and ranked sixth in the nation with 12 saves in 1996. He allowed no runs in 22 of his 25 appearances, stranding 21 of the 26 base runners he inherited. Against MAC teams, he was a perfect seven-for-seven in save opportunities while posting a 0.63 earned run average. He was named to the All-America third team, the All-Mideast Region first team, the All-MAC first team, the Academic All-America third team, the Academic All-District Five team for the second consecutive season and the Academic All-MAC first team.

Bruce Stanley was selected in the Major League Baseball draft three times—after his high school graduation by the Pittsburgh Pirates in the 40th round, after his junior season at Ball State by the Baltimore Orioles in the 11th round, and after his final collegiate campaign by the Kansas City Royals in the 18th round—but never signed. Stanley joined Nick Witte in 1996 to become Ball State's first pitchers to make the All-Mid-American Conference first team. Stanley, who made the All-MAC second team in 1997, owns the Ball State record for most starts in a season with 20 in 1997.

Ed Farris in 1996 became Ball State's second Mid-American Conference Player of the Year after he hit .377 with 15 home runs and 47 runs-batted-in. The infielder received All-America honorable mention and was voted to the All-Mideast Region second team and the All-MAC first team. As a senior, he hit .313 with a league-best 18 homers and 63 RBI to earn All-MAC second-team selection. He made the All-MAC Tournament Team after hitting .429 with two homers, three doubles and nine RBI in three games. He set a Ball State record by crushing three home runs in a 9-2 victory over Fairleigh Dickinson on March 8, 1997. Farris was drafted in the 27th round by the Oakland Athletics in 1997.

After playing third base for Ball State for three years and earning All-Mid-American Conference first-team honors as a junior, Brian Dorrmann moved to shortstop as a senior in 1998 and repeated on the all-league second team. He also made the All-MAC Tournament Team in 1997 and was named the Cardinals' most valuable player in 1998. Dorrmann was among the most difficult batters in the country to strike out for three straight years. In 1996, he ranked 12th, striking out once every 22.65 at-bats. In 1997, he placed 14th, whiffing once every 18 at-bats. In 1998, he climbed to 10th, fanning once every 26.75 at-bats.

As a freshman in 1995, Sam McConnell earned the rare distinction of being selected both pitcher of the year and rookie of the year. He accumulated a career-best five complete games that spring. He produced his best pitching record in 1997, when he was 7-2. His best single-season earned run average was 3.95 in 1996. McConnell was selected in the 11th round of the 1997 Major League Baseball draft by the Pittsburgh Pirates.

Justin Love established Ball State's single-season stolen base record in 1997 with 44 thefts, which led the Mid-American Conference and helped him earn a berth on the all-league second team. That season against Eastern Michigan, Love swiped five bases in five attempts to set a school mark. As a senior in 1998, the center fielder had 30 stolen bases, which ranked second in the conference. He led the league with 62 runs scored and ranked sixth with 120 total bases. Love, an All-MAC first-team pick that season, also was tied for 10th in the conference with nine home runs and a .433 on-base percentage.

Shortstop Jason Murray raised his batting average 138 points between his junior and senior seasons, going from .287 in 1996 to .425 in 1997. His .425 batting average ranked 20th nationally and second in the Mid-American Conference, and it's the sixth highest in Ball State history. His 20 doubles ranked fourth in the conference. He tied a school record with three doubles versus Miami University on April 19. Murray was voted to both the All-Mideast Region and All-Mid-American Conference first teams during his senior season. In 1996, he assisted in four double plays in a single game against Kent State on May 4. In 2002, Murray joined former BSU coach Rich Maloney's staff at Michigan.

Jason Meier enjoyed an all-around All-America season in 1997, as he earned third-team All-America honors and second-team Academic All-American selection. The outfielder was also chosen to the All-Mideast Region and the Academic All-Dictrict Five first teams. He was a member of both the All-Mid-American Conference and Academic All-MAC first teams. He was named the Louisville Slugger National Player of the Week and MAC Hitter of the Week when he batted .550 and had a 1.100 slugging percentage March 31 through April 6, 1997. He set a MAC record that week with 10 runs-batted-in in a game against Valparaiso. Meier finished the season with a .415 batting average, 15 home runs and 65 RBI.

At 6 feet 10 inches, Chris Cabaj, who pitched for Ball State from 1996 to 1999, shares with Southern Cal's Randy Johnson the distinction of being the tallest starting pitchers in NCAA Division I-A history. Cabaj was an All-Mid-American Conference second-team choice in 1998, when he registered an 8-3 record with a 3.44 earned run average. Cabaj was also a two-time Academic All-Mid-American Conference choice. He was selected MAC Pitcher of the Week twice and MAC Scholar-Athlete of the Week once. In 1999, Cabaj was 7-2 with a 4.86 ERA, striking out 80 batters and walking just 14 in 76 innings. He was selected by the Kansas City Royals in the 25th round of the 1999 Major League Baseball draft.

At 6 feet 8 inches, Jeff Urban combined with 6-foot-10-inch Chris Cabaj to give Ball State the tallest pitching duo in collegiate baseball in 1998. The left-handed Urban ranked second in the Mid-American Conference and 28th in the nation with a 2.79 earned run average that season, striking out 78 and walking 22 in 80 2/3 innings. The All-MAC second-team choice managed an 8-3 record that season and finished his career with a 12-4 mark. He struck out a career-high 14 batters in a 5-0 shutout of IUPUI on March 22, 1998. Urban was a supplemental pick between the first and second rounds of the 1998 draft, going to the San Francisco Giants.

Larry Bigbie receives a handshake from coach Rich Maloney as he heads to home plate after hitting a home run. The left-handed right fielder was selected to the All-Mid-American Conference first team in both 1998 and 1999 after being named MAC freshman of the year in 1997. As a senior, Bigbie ranked 24th in the nation with a .419 batting average, which led the league. He also ranked first in the conference with 88 hits, a .514 on-base percentage, 71 runs scored, a .748 slugging percentage and 157 total bases. He was also fourth in stolen bases with 21 and seventh in runs-batted-in with 54.

Left: Larry Bigbie boasts the best career batting average in Ball State history with a .386 mark. He also produced the longest hitting streak—24 games from March 8 to April 18, 1999. His 71 runs scored in 1999 is a single season record for a Cardinal.

Right: Jon Kessick was an All-Mid-American Conference second-team choice in both 1998 and 1999. As a sophomore, he hit .314 with five home runs and 30 runs-batted-in. The following campaign, he batted .337 with nine homers and 38 RBI.

Travis Minix became the first Ball State pitcher to be named to the All-Mid-American Conference first team twice, as he earned the honor in both 1998 and 1999. He set a Ball State single-season record for wins with nine in 1998 and 11 in 1999. As a sophomore, he was 9-2 with a 3.21 earned run average. Minix led the league with 89 strikeouts, while his win total tied for second and his ERA ranked fourth. As a junior, the right-hander was 11-2 with a 2.60 earned run average. The ERA ranked 28th in the country. He finished second in the league with 106 strikeouts and tied for second in wins. Minix was the 23rd-round pick of the Tampa Bay Devil Rays in 1999.

Despite appearing in 15 games and starting 11 in 2000, left-handed pitcher Jason Hickman recorded only two decisions during the season—both victories. He registered a 4.14 earned run average and struck out 53 batters in 63 innings. Following the campaign, he was the eighth-round pick of the Los Angeles Dodgers in the Major League draft. Hickman had also been drafted the year before—by the San Francisco Giants in the 42nd round—after he posted a 2-2 mark.

Matt Wood was selected as a Louisville Slugger National Player of the Week for March 29-April 4, 1999, after he blasted five home runs in the span of nine at-bats to help Ball State to a 5-0 record. The left-handed hitting first baseman batted .600 for the week (nine for 15) with nine runs scored and 16 runs-batted-in. Wood owns the Ball State career home run record with 49 and both the single-season and career marks for RBI with 71 and 221, respectively. Wood, a first-team All-Mid-American Conference selection in 2001 and a second-team All-MAC choice in 1999, was also an Academic All-District Five and Academic All-MAC choice in 1999.

Identical twins Shayne and Jeremy Ridley formed Ball State's double-play combination in 1999 and 2000, with Shayne at shortstop and Jeremy at second base. Both switch-hitters, Jeremy and Shayne finished their four-year careers with amazingly similar statistics. Shayne batted .334 with 33 home runs and 155 runs-batted-in. Jeremy hit .330 with 31 home runs and 165 RBI. Jeremy was selected to the All-America third team in 1999. Both received All-Mideast Region first-team honors, Jeremy in 1999 and Shayne in 2000. Shayne was the Mid-American Conference Player of the Year in 2000 and made the All-MAC first team in 1999 and 2000. Jeremy earned All-MAC first-team selection in 1999. Jeremy was selected to both the Academic All-District Five and the Academic All-Mid-American Conference teams in 1998 and 1999. Shayne was named the MAC Hitter of the Week for April 12-19, 1999. Jeremy was selected the MAC Scholar-Athlete of the Week for March 30-April 4, 1998. Jeremy and Shayne, who graduated from high school in Milton, Ontario, are the sons of Jim Ridley, a scout for the Toronto Blue Jays. Both players were selected in the 2000 Major League Baseball draft, with Shayne going to the Baltimore Orioles in the 19th round and Jeremy to the Blue Jays in the 34th round.

Jeremy Ridley set Ball State records with 194 runs scored, 775 at-bats, 221 games started and 538 assists from 1997 to 2000. Ridley enjoyed his best season in 1999, when he hit .383 with 12 home runs and 68 runs-batted-in. That season, he placed in the top five in the league in seven offensive categories, including second in both hits with 85 and runs-batted-in with 68. The RBI total tied for the fourth highest in MAC history. On April 11, 1999, at Ohio University, Ridley slammed two three-run homers—the first right-handed and the second left-handed—and added a run-scoring single for a career-high seven runs-batted-in.

Shayne Ridley ranked seventh in the nation in 2000 with a .434 batting average, the fourth-highest mark in Ball State history. He also led the league that season with a .495 on-base percentage and a .765 slugging percentage. In 1999, he hit .342—106 points better than the previous campaign—and had career highs with 16 home runs and 62 runs-batted-in. He smacked home runs from both sides of the plate in a 10-0 victory over Miami on April 14. In a championship-clinching doubleheader at Central Michigan on May 15, 1999, he hit three home runs. He twice had 17-game hitting streaks.

Matt Speicher set the Mid-American Conference and Ball State career records with 93 pitching appearances from 1996 to 1999. The right-handed relief pitcher also finished second in BSU history and fourth on the MAC's all-time list with 18 career saves. He was selected to the All-MAC first team in 1998 and the second team in 1999. He tied for the MAC lead in saves with eight in 1998 and ranked second in 1999 with six. In 1997, he ranked 12th in the Mid-American Conference with a 4.30 earned run average.

Chad Wells was the Mid-American Conference Pitcher of the Week for April 17-23, 2000, when he posted a 2-0 record and an 0.76 earned run average. First, he was the winning pitcher in Ball State's 7-3 victory over Butler, and then he threw a complete-game against Northern Illinois, shutting out the Huskies in a 3-0 win. In 12 innings, Wells struck out 12 and walked one. Wells was named to the All-MAC second team in 2000 after posting a 6-4 record with a 3.38 earned run average. In 58 2/3 innings, he struck out 79 while walking just 14.

Aaron Zehnal hit a school-record three home runs in Ball State's 20-7 victory over the Toledo Rockets on April 1, 2001. Zehnal's first homer was a two-run blast over the right field fence in the fifth inning. His second blast came in the seventh inning when he slammed another two-run homer over the right-center field fence. Zehnal's final homer of the game was a three-run smash over the right-center field fence in the eighth inning. In 1998, the outfielder received honorable mention on the Louisville Slugger Freshman All-America team after he batted .309 with seven home runs and 40 runs-batted-in.

Tim Fitzharris fell two hits short of the Mid-American Conference and Ball State career record for hits, when he amassed 257 from 1996 to 2000. He did set the MAC and BSU marks for both career at-bats with 773 and single-season at-bats with 235 in 1999. He finished fifth in league history with 173 career runs and 45 career doubles. He was named to the All-Mid-American Conference second team in 1997 and received honorable mention on the Mizuno Freshman All-America Team in 1996. Fitzharris, who played catcher, first base, third base and the outfield for the Cardinals, had a .334 career batting average.

Pitcher Justin Wechsler became the first Ball State athlete in any sport to earn All-America honors on two different teams as a freshman. In 1999, the right-hander made the Louisville Slugger Freshman All-America first team and the Baseball America Freshman All-America second team. He was also named the MAC Freshman of the Year that season after he recorded a 10-3 record with a 3.39 earned run average and ranked fourth in the league with 64 strikeouts. Wechsler made the All-MAC second team in 1999 and 2001. Wechsler was chosen by the Arizona Diamondbacks in the fourth round of the 2001 Major League Baseball draft.

Jason Paul was voted to the All-Mid-American Conference first team in 2001 after he tied for first in the league with a school record-tying 11 victories and ranked first with a 2.89 earned run average. He also tied for third in games started with 14, ranked fifth in innings pitched with 96 2/3 and finished eighth in strikeouts with 78. He also earned a spot on the MAC All-Tournament Team that spring after he pitched Ball State to an 8-2 victory over Bowling Green and a 6-0 verdict over Central Michigan. Paul was drafted in the 49th round of the 2001 Major League Baseball Draft but decided to return to Ball State for his senior season.

Scott French batted over .300 for four straight years from 1999 to 2002 for Ball State with a high of .330 during his junior campaign. That season, he tied for third in the league with a school record-tying 45 walks and shared fourth with five triples. As a senior, he ranked fifth in the Mid-American Conference with 37 walks and eighth with 16 stolen bases. French set the Ball State career record for walks with 139. He was named to the All-MAC Tournament Team in 2001 after collecting seven hits in 15 at-bats with two home runs and five runs-batted-in. French made most of his 159 career starts in the outfield, but he also pitched and played first base.

Catcher Doug Boone was selected in the 15th round of the 2001 Major League Baseball draft by the Florida Marlins but returned to Ball State for his senior season. He was then drafted in the 36th round by the New York Yankees. In 2000, Boone was named to the All-Mid-American Conference Tournament Team after slugging two home runs in four games, including the game-winner against Central Michigan on May 19. Boone enjoyed his best offensive season in 2000, when he hit .289 with 12 home runs and 38 runs-batted-in—all career highs.

Bryan Bullington became the first Mid-American Conference athlete in any sport to be the overall No. 1 selection in a professional league's draft when the Pittsburgh Pirates drafted him after his junior season in 2002. The right-handed pitcher was a consensus All-American in 2002, being chosen by the American Baseball Coaches Association, Baseball America, Collegiate Baseball/Louisville Slugger and the National Collegiate Baseball Writers Association. The NCBWA named him the District Five Player of the Year, and he made the All-Mideast Region first team for the third straight season. The NCBWA also named him national pitcher of the week for April 8-14, 2002. Bullington was the Mid-American Conference Pitcher of the Year in both 2001 and 2002, and he was All-MAC first team all three of his campaigns at Ball State. He was also selected to the Academic All-District Five team in 2002. He played on the 2001 USA National Team. In 2000, he was voted the Mid-American Conference Freshman of the Year and was named to the Louisville Slugger Freshman All-America Team and the Baseball-America Freshman All-America second team.

Bryan Bullington set Mid-American Conference strikeout records with 357 in his career and 139 in one season. In 2002, the 6-foot-5-inch hurler ranked sixth in the nation with an average of 11.9 strikeouts per nine innings. He ranked first in the Mid-American Conference with a 2.84 earned run average, 139 strikeouts, 11 victories and 104 2/3 innings pitched. As a sophomore, Bullington led the conference with 119 strikeouts and nine victories. During his freshman campaign, he was No. 1 in the league in strikeouts with 99 and tied for first in victories with nine.

After being selected No. 1 in the 2002 Major League draft, Bryan Bullington is interviewed by an Indianapolis television reporter at his family's home in Fishers, Indiana. All four members of Bullington's family attended Ball State. His father, Larry, was a three-year letterman in both baseball and basketball for the Cardinals, and his mother, Mary, was a swimmer at the university before receiving their degrees. Bryan's sister, Megan, graduated from Ball State in 2002.

Left: Matt Deckman became Ball State's second two-time Academic All-American when he was named to the first team in 2002 after earning third-team selection in 2001. He also earned Academic All-District Five honors both seasons. He graduated from Ball State with a 3.93 grade point average on Ball State's 4.0 scale with a degree in exercise science. In 2001, Deckman received the National Amateur Baseball Federation Scholarship Award.

Middle: Matt Deckman was named to the All-Mid-American Conference second team in 2002 after ranking ninth in the league in both hitting with a .383 batting average and on-base percentage with a .465 mark. He shared Ball State's most valuable player award with Bryan Bullington and received the Cardinals' best-defensive-player award. On April 24 against Butler, he tied a school record by participating in four double plays.

Right: Paul Henry was named to the 2001 American Baseball Coaches Association All-America third team after the shortstop hit .400 with 12 home runs and 62 runs-batted-in plus accumulated eight saves as a relief pitcher. He also was named to the All-Mid-American Conference first team and the ABCA All-Mideast Region team that season. As a senior, Henry made both the All-MAC and All-Mideast Region second teams after batting .332 with 12 homers and 59 RBI, and collecting three saves. Henry went in the seventh round of the 2002 Major League Baseball draft to the Baltimore Orioles.

Ball State's most-improved-player award in 2002 was no surprise. After pitching just over 41 innings in his first two seasons at Ball State, pitcher Luke Hagerty earned a spot on the All-Mid-American Conference first team that season. Then he became the 32nd overall selection in the Major League Baseball draft, going to the Chicago Cubs as a supplemental pick between the first and second rounds. The 6-foot-8-inch left-hander also made the All-Mideast Region second team in 2002. In conference rankings for the season, Hagerty finished first with seven complete games, second with a 3.02 earned run average and tied for third with seven wins.

Appendix A

Baseball Players and Coaches in the Ball State Athletic Hall of Fame

Name	Year Inducted
Ray Louthen	1976
Merv Rettenmund	1976
Virgil Schooler	1976
Billy Williams	1976
Rex Rudicel	1977
Wayne Van Sickle	1980
John Brogneaux	1982
Walter Pesavento	1982
Marvin Heaton	1983
Larry Bullington	1984
Jim Roudebush	1984
Bob Heady	1985
Frank Houk	1985
Gabor Takats	1985
Curtis Rathburn	1986
Homer Jackson	1987
Mike Readnour	1987
Art Yaroch	1988
Ed Sherry	1990
Ernie Sutton	1991
Ted Huber	1993
Vic Overman	1994
Rick Morrison	1995
Thomas Howard	1996
Bill Reynolds	1996
Mark Davis	2001

Appendix B

Ball State baseball lettermen

whose names do not appear elsewhere in this book:

Forrest Albright
Jeff Alexander (mgr.)
Mike Anderson
Richard Apple
Tony Arasi
Charles Arch
Chas Arch
Scott Archibald
John Armington
Bob Bachman
Rick Bailey
George Baird
Ron Baldwin
Kevin Barnes
James Barron
Greg Bartlett
Tom Barwise
Bill Baugh
Richard Beck
Keith Becker
Mitch Bedree
Roger Beehler
Jerry Beeman (mgr.)
Robert Belangee
Craig Benbow
Kyle Benbow
Bob Bennett (mgr.)
Scott Bienz
Donald Bivens
Hubert Blair
Floyd Blake
Brent Bleh
Perry Blessing (mgr.)
Maynard Bough
Tony Bowen
Joe Boyd
Ted Bragg
A.F. Brainard
Dick Brainerd
Aaron Breehne
Burt Brenneman (mgr.)
Joseph Briggs
John Brill
Kirk Brotherton
Harold Brubaker
William Bryan
Scott Bryson
Kory Bucklew
Leonard Buczkowski
Matt Bullock
Travis Burleson
Robert Burns
Fred Burt
Ralph Bushey
Gary Caldwell
Greg Campbell
Jim Campbell
Larry Campbell
Marshall Campbell
Carl Carmichael
Gilbert Carpenter
David Carr
John Cate
Jon Cave
Tony Christopher
Glenn Church (mgr.)
Charles Cizek
James Clark
Scott Cochran
Warren Colglazier
Dick Collins
John Cooper
Rick Cooper
Jason Cosby
James Coughlin
Justin Crews
Larry Cripe
Justin Crowell
Paul Curtis
Bill Danner
Chad Daugherty
Chris Dauss (mgr.)
Paul Davis
Rex Decker
Pat Dejulia
Kenneth Delk
Trent Dewees
Don Dick
Dorwin Dick
Marvin Dick
Otto Dickerson
Brad Dobbs
Kenneth Dubie
Brandon Duvall
David Duvnjak
Tom Dyer (mgr.)
Rick Eads
Joe Elliott
Joe Eylens
Leon Fadley
Denny Farner
Mike Fernandez
Don Fickert
Jim Fields
Bill Fisher
Alan Fitzgerald
Tim Fitzgerald
Duane Foist (mgr.)
Lamoile Ford (mgr.)
Todd Fox
Alan Fozo
Jim Frank
Tim Frank
Marc Franz
Ervin Fratus
James Fravel
Lucas Fry
Harry Fullerton
Gerald Gerard
Dave Gilbert
Ross Giusti
Fred Glancy
Barry Godown
John Good
Howard Gooden
Marvin Gordon (mgr.)
Wesley Gough
John Graham
Kenton Granger
Kevin Green
Ralph Grimme
H. Groininger
Reed Groininger
John Gunn (mgr.)
Burdette Hall
Jim Hamilton
Rich Hammond (mgr.)
George Harding
Cecil Harrell
Jeff Harrell
Theodore Harris
Brad Hart
LaVerne Hartley
Gary Hartnagel
Jeff Hartnagel
George Harvey
Joe Harvey
Norman Haverkos
Mike Haviland
Kenneth Hayette
Clyde Hays
Edwin Heifner
J.D. Heilmann
Dick Henderson (mgr.)
Mike Hennie
Bert Hensley
John Hess
Al Heuss
Estel Hiatt
Chris Himsel
Tim Hines
Max Hobbs (mgr.)
William Hofmann
Perce Hoffner
Jeff Holcomb
Don Huffer
Jim Hughes
Joe Humkey (mgr.)
Ernest Hurt
Cleon Hutchison
Harold Hutchison
Jim Irwin
Randy Jobe
Steve Johnson
Brad Johnston
Brad Jones
Robert Jones (mgr.)
Warren Jones
Matthew Joris
Clifford Joyce
Harry Justus
Richard Keithley
Richard Keller (mgr.)
Arley Kerr
Herschell King
Chris Kinnett (mgr.)
Carl Kirkman
Frank Kitchel (mgr.)
Sam Kitchens
John Kite
Matt Knisely
Ned Koning
Robert Koontz
Steve Krah (mgr.)
Brian Kruse
James Kunnen
Chris Landrigan
Scott Larsen (mgr.)
Kent Lebherz
John Lebo
Greg Lee
Mike Lehrman
Joseph Lewis
Jack Liggett
Clarence Lindzy
Ray Linson
Bob Loft (Mgr.)
Harold Long
Wendell Long
Raymond Loveless
Bob Lowder
John Ludwig
Rodger Macy
Matt Mairn
Richard Marr (mgr.)
David Martin
Joe Mason
Ken Mathis
Stewart Mattix
Kevin Maxwell
Ed May
Collin McAtee
Phillip McCarter
William McColly
Chris McCoy
Jim McWilliams (mgr.)
Gene Miller (mgr.)
Jeff Miller
Guy Millikan
Dave Minnich
Paul Minnich
Jerry Moore
Tom Morris
John Neff (mgr.)
Erik Niehaus
Steve Niehaus
Greg Nix
Tony Nukes
Jason Ogle
Larry Orban
Tim O'Reilly
Danny Orem
Don Oren
Tom Overstreet
Neal Packanik
Joe Parker
Marvin Pazdol
Bill Peden (mgr.)
Myron Peebles
Michael Penn
Richard Peterson
Joe Pickard (mgr.)
Mike Pierce
Larry Pinkerton
Jim Ponto
Rick Ponto
Perry Powers
Willis Preston
Richard Price
Mike Putnam
Jeff Quinn
Vince Rago
Joseph Rapp (mgr.)
Vaughn Redding
Floyd Reed
Merritt Reed
Francis Rees
Leslie Reeves
Jan Relford
Dave Restau
Earl Richardson
Bob Richey
Larry Richey
Rick Richmond
Ralph Rigdon
Pete Riggle
Steve Rinker
Bill Ritchie
Gerald Roach
Jud Robinett
Rickey Robinson
Brent Rodenbeck
Paul Royko
Waldo Sauter
Rudy Schaumburg
Eugene Schnyder
Mark Schoeff (mgr.)
Ben Schroeder
Mike Schuck
Jake Schuman
Stuart Scott
Steve Seager
Jim Seamon
Jack Sell (Mgr.)
Ken Sendre (mgr.)
Oris Shanks
Orrin Shaw
Adam Sheefel
Dean Shepard
Dan Sheilds
Everett Shively
John Shively
Jerry Shuck
Al Shumm
Frank Sigler
Brian Simmons
Wally Simpson
Carwyn Singleton (mgr.)
Paul Sloan (mgr.)
Bonnie Smith
Bret Smith
George Smith
Terry Smith
R. Nelson Snider
Larry Snyder
Ron Snyder
John Squires
Charles Stoker
W. Stoner (mgr.)
Craig Stoops
Howard Stout
Marvin Stout
David Stralkowski
Robert Streelman
Kevin Sublette (mgr.)
Phil Summer
Richard Surowiec
Dave Taylor
Mike Terveer
Almon Thompson
Lance Tigyer
Jack Titus
Charles Toler
Ron Toll (mgr.)
Lloyd Townsend (mgr.)
Randy Ude
Ward Underwood
Mike Urban
Dan Vandergrift
D.J. Van Keuren
Rolland Van Skyock
Jim Vineyard
Bill Waddell
Sherman Waggoner
John Walker
Shirley Wasson
Roy Watson
Scott Wessel
Don Whalen
A. Edward White
Ken Williams
Louis Williams
Jason Willis
Tim Wills
Brad Wilson
John Wilson
Mike Wood
Tom Wylie
Mark Yates
Jason York
Henry Zawacki
Glendon Zinser